I0577523

The Sailor's World

The Sail

Photography by Stanley Rosenfeld

or's World

by Arthur Beiser

A Ridge Press Book / Random House, New York

Editor-in-Chief: Jerry Mason
Editor: Adolph Suehsdorf
Art Director: Albert Squillace
Associate Editor: Moira Duggan
Associate Editor: Barbara Hoffbeck
Art Associate: Mark Liebergall
Art Production: Doris Mullane

Picture Credits
All photographs are by Stanley Rosenfeld except the following:
Arthur Beiser—43 right, 86 upper right, 150 bottom,
159 right, 175 top, 195 upper left, 203 upper left & bottom,
206 bottom, 214 bottom left, 215 bottom right, 223 top left & right,
236 top left & middle left
Beken of Cowes—51 left, 185
Porter Buck—234
Ted Kelly—81 bottom
Alfred Levy—186 top
Red Marston—81 top
Bill Robinson—182, 184, 188, 189, 215 top, 223 bottom, 236 right

The Sailor's World *by Arthur Beiser*
First printing.
All rights reserved.
Published in the United States by Random House, New York, and
simultaneously in Canada by Random House of Canada, Limited, Toronto.
Prepared and produced by The Ridge Press, Inc.
Library of Congress Catalog Card Number: 78-183593
ISBN: 0-394-46852-X
Printed and bound in Italy by Mondadori Editore, Verona.

To my past and future shipmates, especially Germaine, Nadia, Alexa, and Isabel

Contents

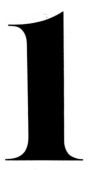

Preface

*Sharing pleasure is itself pleasure, which is why I
have enjoyed writing this book. If through its words I am able
to seduce readers into going sailing for the first time,
I shall feel well rewarded. If I can lure Sunday sailors into tasting
the stronger wine of racing and cruising, I shall be more
than pleased. And if someone should venture forth to track the
setting sun to its lair with his resolution fortified by
anything I have said, my cup of delight will run over. Before
going further, I think it proper to admit that, unlike
most people who write books on sailing, nothing I have done at sea
has been in the least exceptional. Nor do I aspire to win
the Bermuda Race, to defend the America's Cup, to cross an ocean
single-handed, or to sail around the world nonstop.
One great thing about sailing is that there are no real rules
of the game, and each participant is free not only to
choose how he will play but also to decide the score by himself
afterward. I regard myself as qualified to write on
sailing because, on the basis of my own method of assessment,
I have a perfect record at sea—whatever it is
I seek (and I am not sure I will ever be able to pin it down),
never yet have I failed to find it in ample measure.
The very freedom that sailing offers tends to make newcomers
feel insecure if they cannot identify specific
goals to achieve. Reading books and articles on sailing only
worsens the situation, for their authors always
seem to know exactly what they want to accomplish. Mountaineers
have summits; sailors, too, would seem obliged to
have some sort of objective in mind. Or must they? Is winning
a race or rounding Cape Horn really any less ephemeral
than a sunny afternoon's trip to wherever the wind is blowing?
It is for the sailor himself to decide. I hope this
book, by the diversity it shows the sailor's world to contain,
will hearten equally those whose quest is for the
best path toward a definite end and those for whom the paths*

themselves represent sufficient end.
Old salts already have settled into congenial
styles of life on the water. What I can perhaps offer them is a
refreshment of memory, an album to which they can
add their own moments of stress and accomplishment. And they
are welcome to amend my perceptions as they like.
It is winter as I write, and where I live nearly all the yachts
have been hauled from the water to await spring.
My own Minots Light *rests in a shed four hundred miles from here,*
her masts drawn, her lockers and tanks empty, a lifeless
shell. April seems far away. This morning I walked down to the
harbor and saw four Solings set out for an informal
race, their hulls bright splashes of color against the gray-green
water. I must have watched similar scenes a thousand
times, yet I found myself rooted to the spot, unable to take my eyes
from the darting forms that converged so exactly
on each mark of the course.
Finally the race was over, and as the boats were maneuvered
in turn under the pierside crane to be lifted into
their trailers, I realized how cold I was and started home.
My thoughts turned to the next season, and tonight
charts will cover the living-room floor, pilot books will be pored
over, and over the next weeks the plans for the
coming summer's cruise will be blocked out. The subtle art of
crimping—subtle these days, anyway—then will take
over to assure appropriate crews for each stage of the voyage.
There will be consultations with the yard, with the
sailmaker, with the chandler, with the chart agent. My wife will
begin filling shelves with hard-to-get items for the larder,
and all of us will start to make lists, lists, lists. The feeling
of loss that came in October when Minots Light *was hauled is*
gone now, and I shall envy no man until next October.

A. B.
Klampenborg, Denmark

1/Sett

ing Sail

ailing is the supreme sport. In fact, it is more like a way of life than a sport. Every aspect of sailing has its own fascination, from one-design racing around the buoys to cruising over the horizon, from fitting out in the spring to the final wet beat in November to the yard for hauling out. Some sailors are blessed with climates that permit them to be on the water the year around, but others in less equable regions are just as happy with the contrasts and opportunities the different seasons bring. To set sail is to embark on an adventure, no matter how often it is done or how familiar the scene. And it is an adventure that never fails to exhilarate the spirit as it challenges the mind and body.

Sailing sharpens the senses and heightens the appetites. Given a whiff of sea air, a splash of the sea itself, and a turn at the helm, the most moribund city dweller blossoms into life. No tonic yet invented compares with a newly launched sailboat at restoring the pulse of youth. The ardor of the returning sailor is no myth, which perhaps is why many a wife tolerates her husband's nautical mistress.

To set out for a sail always fills me with a surge of well-being. The feeling is partly relief at leaving behind the cares of the shore, partly anticipation of the excitement to come. But there is also a deeper undercurrent of some primordial lust for the sea, a curious sensation (for I am of pure landlubber stock) of being at home at last. Every dedicated sailor I know experiences a similar access of emotion as he casts off docking lines or mooring pennant and swings out under the press of the mainsail.

Once clear of the shore, sails up and the helm alive, it is time to make decisions. Where to go has already been decided, unless what is in mind is a day sail just for the not-inconsiderable hell of it. Now tactics must be devised for the strategy chosen. Would it be better to hug the shore to avoid the brunt of the tidal stream, or to head boldly out in the hope of more wind? Which is the better tack, taking into account the benefits of having any current present on the lee bow and the possibilities of wind shifts later? If the initial course is downwind, should the

Opening pages: 73-foot ketch
Jubilee off Block Island
soon after start of 1970 Bermuda
Race. A reef has been rolled
in mizzen to ease helm in vigorous
southwesterly breeze.
No adventure could have more
auspicious beginning.

spinnaker be set (his pulse quickens), or would it be more sensible to tack downwind without it (she starts to breathe again)?

If a race is in store, the questions are different. Which end of the starting line is more favorable? Would timed runs to the line be a good idea? Which skipper has been having a run of luck—he would consider it a flowering of talent, the egotistical bastard —in gauging wind shifts and tidal quirks lately? There is always plenty to think about under sail, but no decision is final and something may arise at any time to turn the situation on its ear. And tomorrow or next week there will be another chance, a good argument for not taking matters so seriously that profit-and-loss calculations exclude the spontaneous element in sailing.

The longer the course, whether cruise or race, the denser the conflicting calculations that accompany the start. But once away, sheets hard and the wake hissing past the counter, all doubts are replaced by solid confidence, the absolute certainty that there is nowhere else that one would rather be.

There is beauty as well as adventure in sailing, and one is as responsible as the other for the satisfaction sailing affords. To begin with, a proper sailboat is a lovely thing in itself. The thrusting bow, the so-slender mast trapped in a web of rigging, the tiller swinging gently as if in quest of a purposeful hand, the elegant lift of the counter; few works of man articulate so many disparate strands into such a harmonious whole.

But the static grace of a moored sailboat is only incidental. With its sails up and freed from its tether, a sailboat comes alive to begin a passionate interplay between sails and wind, hull and sea. The essence of sailing is a knife-edge balance between defying nature and yielding to it. To participate in maintaining this balance, even to witness it, is an aesthetic experience of the highest order.

Where do powerboats fit into the picture? After all, sailing is a complex and subtle art whose mastery permits one to go at hardly more than a donkey's pace, often not even in the desired direction, whereas a powerboat goes where it is pointed at a two-digit speed. As a means of transport, a powerboat certainly makes sense. However,

13

Watching sailboats race may be
no more exciting than watching grass
grow, but to participants it
is another story. *Opposite: One-design
sloops on Long Island Sound.
Above: Handicap racing off Block Island.
Left: The larger the boat,
the larger the crew needed to race it.*

as a means of entering into communion with the natural world, as a medium of personal expression, even as a way to enjoy an afternoon, a powerboat leaves me unimpressed. Whenever a powerboat goes past with a roar of exhaust and a heedless wake, I feel pity for the owner whose ego needs boosting in this way. A powerboat in a garden of islands is as much an intruder as a motorcycle in a garden of flowers.

Different people enjoy different kinds of sailing. The tense figure at the helm of an ocean racer that is staggering under the thrust of the nylon bubble of its spinnaker does not envy his counterpart slouched quite happily in the cockpit of a cruising ketch that is loping off more sedately under plain sail, and neither of them would trade places with the gymnast out on the trapeze of a Flying Dutchman, who, in his turn, watches the others with a smile of amused contempt.

What kind of sailing suits a given person is largely a matter of taste. The only way to find out is to try everything. And tastes change with experience, so the uncertain beginner who is happiest on a day

sailer in protected waters may end up breathing fire on the foredeck of a 12-meter or collecting flying fish for breakfast from the deck of a vessel in the trade winds.

The two chief approaches to learning the art of sailing are, first, to go out in charge of a small boat from the start, and, second, to crew in a large boat under expert direction. These approaches are really complementary, not competitive. Being in command of a ship, any ship, develops initiative, foresight, and self-confidence, but adds little to skill once past the rudiments. Crewing on a well-organized boat brings quick sophistication, but not much scope for experiment. One must do both.

Sailing schools are good for the complete novice, but a course lasting a week or two is hardly enough for more than an introduction. The next step, or perhaps the first one if no school is nearby, is somehow to gain access to a small and a large sailboat.

The folklore of sailing has it that one should start out by mastering a dinghy and only afterward ascend to the majesty of a keelboat. I suppose the theory here is that if a mistake means a knockdown or

17

Light airs test skill and patience
of the sailor. Here 48-foot
cutter Thunderhead *extracts every*
possible ounce of propulsion
from kittenish breeze on Long Island
Sound. Designed by Philip
Rhodes, clipper-bowed Thunderhead *was*
built by Abeking & Rasmussen.

a capsize, the novice will learn fast. I think this is nonsense which has needlessly turned many people away from sailing.

The right way to learn the skipper's trade is to sail in a stable, docile craft which rewards skill but shrugs off incompetence. There are plenty of such boats around, and in most yachting centers they can be bought, or rented by the day or week. Each area has its own favorites. The way to make a sensible choice is to ask local sailors (not dealers) and to go for trial spins to see how the most likely candidates behave. Be sure to get a fast boat—though it need not *look* fast—not a clunker.

To master the technical details of sailing, one should crew on the largest well-run boat on which a berth can be wangled. On a small boat it is easy to clear almost any snarl that occurs, and in consequence corners are likely to be cut in handling sail, in pilotage, in docking, and so forth. On a large boat no corners can be cut, literally or figuratively. Everything must be done right the first time, with the foredeck and cockpit hands meshing their efforts precisely. Going aground is not amusing, nor is bashing into a dock. Forces measured in tens of pounds on a dinghy and in hundreds of pounds on a small auxiliary are measured in tons on a large sailboat, and, except in light airs, analysis, not improvisation, governs every action.

Very well, agreed that the thing to do is to crew on a big boat and gather expertise with one's head rather than with the seat of one's pants. Easy enough to say, but who in his right mind will take on a beginner as crew? It is true that anybody who has sunk tens or hundreds of thousands of dollars in a boat and who knows how to handle it properly prefers an expert crew. But expert crews are hard to find and harder to keep. After a tour as crew on another man's boat, many people want one of their own, however smaller or less able. So there is a constant turnover. And not all members of a crew are on tap whenever the owner decides to go on a race or a cruise or for a day sail. Most owners would be only too pleased to have a few willing hands, even if inexperienced, to back up their regular crews. And if the tyro offers help with maintenance during the season, which is in any case an opportunity to gain invaluable knowledge, he

To venture in harmony with
natural world to distant places
is goal of cruising sailor.
No trophy awaits arrival of this
ketch wherever it is bound,
but memory of this evening will
need no polishing to remain
bright in memories of her crew.

will be all the more welcome.

The way to begin is to somehow get introduced to the owner of a suitable boat and then soften him up by admiring the boat. Ask any woman for pointers on these preliminaries, but be sure not to call his sloop a yawl or commit any other unforgivable blunder. If you are a woman, short fingernails will add realism to your story; a short skirt won't hurt, either. No matter how uninterested the owner seems at the time, give him your name, address, and phone number on a piece of paper. Unless you have two heads or a sixty-inch waistline, the chances are he will keep the paper and someday give you a ring.

Given a choice, should one prefer a berth for a cruise or for a race? This is hard to say. Some cruising skippers are just as keen at getting the most from their vessels as any racing man, and in addition a cruise normally involves a broader spectrum of activities than a race does. Still, a race means competition and hence is bound to be a more concentrated venture. A race also means a fixed course with no concessions to the weather, and a nasty day on which the

cruising man samples the joys of lying at anchor has his racing cousin out there taking a dusting.

By and large, women do not enjoy sailing as much as men do. Much of the trouble, I believe, can be traced to feelings of inadequacy, fears of not being up to the demands of what might happen under way. Yet very little of sailing requires physical strength as such, and women who come to sailing with open minds often become competent sailors as devoted to the sport as any man.

One thing many women resent is being consigned to the galley. The profession of cook is a noble one, and it is hard to understand why anybody would want to forgo the deluge of affection that inundates the author of a good meal at sea. I grant that a talented cook will be infuriated at times by the lack of discrimination her constituency exhibits; my wife, a superb cook on and off the water, is maddened by the preference sailors tend to have for quantity over quality, for speed over finesse. On the other hand even the worst cook can make peanut-butter sandwiches and heat cans of soup, which if done

21

Sailing comes in a variety
of packages to suit every taste
and bank account. Left:
Crew of Tempest-class keel sloop
uses trapeze to keep it
level on a beat. Below: Sailfish
provides simple and
cheap, if wet, way to enjoy sailing.

at the right time will have a boatload of hearties at her feet.

But women are also useful on deck, regardless of their role in the galley. My wife is better at steering to windward than any man I know, and I am sad that, after a couple of unfortunate spinnaker wraps and a Chinese jibe long ago, she is still nervous about taking the helm downwind. My daughters love sail handling and are eager students of sail trim, and I think they take as much pleasure in carrying out the various jobs assigned to them as I take in watching their growing expertise. It is all a matter of assigning an appropriate degree of responsibility and taking the results seriously.

I hope the above remarks do not seem patronizing, for I do not mean them that way. It is just that many women regard sailing as a man's game, and they need to be coaxed into responding to it.

Sailing, then, is for the whole woman as well as for the whole man, good clean fun on deck and good dirty fun down below for both. No woman should allow herself to be stuck in the galley while Jack Armstrong hogs the helm, nor should she wash dishes on a velvet night when a gibbous moon pleads to draw fire from a ruby in her navel.

Sailing offers a host of subsidiary pleasures to supplement the more obvious ones. I always enjoy meeting and talking with other sailors, for example. Whatever it is that calls people to sailing seems to choose those with personal style and substance; and I don't mean financial substance in this respect. Rich or poor, it's good to have money, but once the money has purchased a sailboat, the distinction disappears on the water. The more remote a harbor, the more interesting the people who sail there, and if the boat is small, the members of its crew are usually more interesting still. I look forward every spring to the company of fellow sailors almost as much as I look forward to grasping the wheel once more to guide *Minots Light* on her first sail of the season.

Another attractive aspect of sailing is its terminology, which baffles at first but becomes a joy to speak and hear on better acquaintance. Every trade has its jargon, but that of the sailor is the most resplendent. How marvelous to begin a voyage by slipping a mooring or weighing anchor, then to beat across a sea of white horses.

Each nautical word has a specific meaning, and the words are different in texture to prevent confusion. Port and starboard, bow and stern, hawsehole and scupper, genoa and spinnaker, tack and jibe, to weather and to lee—to listen to sailors talk is to hear arabesques of language the more vivid for their economy and precision.

Besides the vocabulary still current there is a bottomless sea chest of other terms worth reviving. I would love to be able to tell someone to hoist the jib cheerily (quickly) or to sheet it in handsomely (slowly and steadily) and have him know what I mean. Hardly anybody makes an offing, sails full and by, or even belays a line any more. Still, splicing the main brace remains a popular expression, though who today knows what a main brace is or why splicing it should be an occasion to fill all hands with Dutch courage?

Sailing is an amalgam of many elements. Peel away the nonessentials, boil down what is left, strain the residue through a fine mesh and you will have at the end a small sloop ghosting out of a harbor soon after sunrise. In the cuddy is a paddle, sandwiches, something to drink, a flashlight, life jackets. Soon two sweaters will join them. In the cockpit one figure holds the tiller lightly and watches for cat's-paws ahead, the other trims the sails to make the most of the nascent breeze. The sun washes away the milky haze of early morning as the boat tacks to clear a headland, then tacks again and is lost to sight.

At dusk the sloop returns, reaching silently past the breakwater. The faces of its occupants are flushed from the sun. A luff and the jib is down, a moment later the mooring is picked up and the mainsail descends as well. The sails are bagged, the cockpit covered, and in the last of the light the dinghy is rowed ashore. Where did they go? Nowhere. Everywhere. What did they accomplish? Nothing. Everything.

Not everyone is able to enjoy such a day. The competitive urge drives many sailors to racing, the lure of adventure attracts others to cruising beyond the horizon. But all sailing is built upon the sensations which are felt by any sailor on a simple boat out for an aimless spin.

25

2/The

Boat

A sailboat is a marvelous object, one of the supreme creations of man. To own the right sailboat for one's temperament is like being married to the right woman: it is a two-way street with devotion flowing in both directions through the years. The catch lies in the qualifying phrase "for one's temperament." Almost every sailboat seems splendid at first glance, whether casual day sailer or Olympic one-design, coastwise cruiser or ocean racer. The problem in buying a boat is not so much to match one's dreams with one's pocketbook as it is to nail down just what those dreams add up to.

Every type of sailboat, if honestly designed and built, gives pleasure of some kind. I only wish I could have one of each to enjoy as my moods shift. There are days on which I feel like aimlessly pottering around in a little sloop like my daughters' *Shenandoah*, other days on which the urge to head my ketch *Minots Light* toward the far horizon becomes overpowering. A casual weekend jaunt with my wife in a smaller boat than *Minots Light* has more than once seemed an attractive idea. Often I wish I owned a Dragon or a Soling and could race every weekend round the buoys on an even basis. Sometimes the competitive instinct and the desire to go far come to the surface simultaneously and the only relief would be to go ocean racing. If you want advice on what kind of boat to buy, don't ask me. I love them all.

But if I can't say what is the best boat, I certainly can say what is the worst, namely the boat meant for more than one basic function. The Soling is a thoroughbred one-design racing boat precisely because that is all Jan Linge had in mind when he designed it. If an attempt had been made to have the Soling also suitable as a day sailer for relaxed fooling around and as an overnight boat with some sort of cabin, the result would have been mediocrity all around. As it is the Soling makes a poor day sailer and a worse cruiser, and is superb for racing.

Similarly, it is impossible to strike a decent compromise between the requirements of cruising and handicap racing. A cruising boat ought to be comfortable,

*Opening pages: All clear to
set spinnaker aboard Tripp-designed,
48-foot centerboard sloop
Katrinka. Well-planned, well-equipped
deck makes brute strength
not necessary for sailing her properly
and windows in hull
contribute to cheerful interior.*

stable, and fast, easy to handle under sail and power, and able to tolerate both an unskilled hand at the helm and the stores for a long passage without sacrificing performance. A racing boat ought to fit the measurement rule like a skin and concede nothing to human frailty when it conflicts with efficiency.

I honestly cannot see any middle ground between the two. It is hard to say which is worse, to sail a race in a basically cruising boat knowing that it is a futile effort, or to cruise in a basically racing boat and be worn out by its spiteful ways and lack of comfort. On the other hand, what a joy to compete in a flat-out racer, to commit every resource of mind, body, and bank account to achieve victory. And what a supremely satisfying experience to undertake a passage in a real cruiser, a free man (for a while) in a world brimming with problems.

Size alone is no measure of a sailboat's merit. Small and large boats alike can approach perfection, each in its own way. Nor is an expensive craft of a given size and type necessarily more satisfactory than a cheap one. It depends upon what the additional money is used to buy. It is easy to double the price and halve the performance of a vessel by installing a mass of equipment whose utility is marginal, or to make it so complicated that all spontaneity is lost when under way.

The majority of sailboats are small and simple, and afford great pleasure at modest cost. For someone who wishes to experience the poetry of action that is sailing in its purest form, such a boat is ideal.

A day sailer or one-design racer becomes an extension of its crew, a willing partner that responds to their will with no conscious effort on their part. Each maneuver, each sail adjustment, seems to carry itself out automatically. To relinquish the tiller and sheets at the end of the day leaves a feeling of incompleteness, like losing a limb. No wonder every harbor on a summer evening is host to sloops that circle round and round after their return, their crews reluctant to break the spell that possesses them.

The big distinction in day boats is between unballasted centerboarders and self-righting keelboats. A modern centerboard dinghy is lively, planes readily, and is easy to transport on a trailer. The crew is

29

Ted Hood designs boats
besides making sails for them.
Of shoal draft and fairly
heavy for size, his various Robins
are as suited to cruising
as to racing. Mizzen spinnaker
is nice to look at
and might even do some good.

the ballast, however, and agility—not to mention wet sweaters and a trapeze—is essential in a gusty wind and poppled sea. An hour in a dinghy under such conditions, skimming the water on the verge of a capsize amid bursts of spray, is incomparable sport.

A keelboat does not rely entirely upon its crew for stability, and by virtue of its greater weight offers a steadier ride. Reactions to wind changes can be slower without penalty, though skilled handling is certainly rewarded. The intellectual element is perhaps more pronounced in keelboat sailing, while the physical element becomes less significant.

Many sailors are entirely happy with day sailing or one-design racing, and ask for no more than the right boat and the right place to sail it for a few hours at a time. Other sailors are harder to satisfy and require the self-sufficiency provided by an enclosed cabin with living accommodations. The unavoidable sacrifice of responsive performance is accepted in exchange for the ability to live aboard while cruising or racing from place to place. In a well-designed boat the sacrifice may be minor, and well

compensated for by the wider horizons that open up.

In my book *The Proper Yacht* I drew a line at roughly thirty-six feet overall as "the lower limit of the size of a proper cruising boat . . . set by the requirements that two people be able to live aboard it for a few weeks at a time and that it be capable of an ocean crossing on its own bottom, both without serious discomfort." These requirements, needless to say, are hardly everybody's, and boats well under thirty-six feet overall can be wholly successful at cruising and handicap racing. And small cruising boats have advantages over large ones when long voyages offshore are not part of the picture: they are easier to manage generally, and are often more fun to sail. Little effort is needed to change jibs or to set a spinnaker on a boat twenty-five or thirty feet long, and such a boat has open to it many harbors and anchorages denied its larger sisters.

A cruising boat of moderate size is ideal as the first boat for a family. Every kind of sailing can be sampled at a cost, in terms of time and effort as well as of money, that is not great. The essential thing

Above: Dragons racing near
Copenhagen. Designed
in 1929, class is still active.
Top left: Solings are
very popular for one-design
racing throughout world.
Left: Handicap racers like
Mustang must take
all weathers in stride.

*Ideal beginner's boat is day
sailer with small cabin.
Cost is modest, rig could not
be simpler, and unlike
more aristocratic cousins
such a boat responds as
well to novice hand on tiller
as to that of expert.*

is to get a boat that actually *sails,* even though the domestic end may be less than perfect; what counts on the water is not what counts at the boat show.

My own first sailboat was a cutter not quite twenty-eight feet long. Her name was *Nipinke,* and I have never had more pleasure from a boat than she provided in the two years I owned her.

Nipinke was designed by Ralph Winslow and built by the same yard (Quincy Adams in Massachusetts) and in the same year (1935) as *Ticonderoga,* but there the resemblance ceased. Her profile was lovely, true, but there was a price, namely crouching headroom in the main cabin, less than that up forward. The main cabin sported two transom berths and in the fore cabin a pipe berth folded down over the head. The galley consisted of an unreliable alcohol stove and a water tap but no sink. The engine was the original one and was covered with rust. Neither lifelines nor pulpit graced the deck, and the only navigational instrument was a compass whose card tended to stick. A 6-foot pram barely fit on the cabin top, but as it covered the companion hatch in this

position it was usually towed at the expense of at least half a knot, a not-inconsiderable fraction of *Nipinke's* normal speed. On a beat in a wind of any weight the upper part of the mast bent alarmingly to leeward and her garboards tended to open up. There was rot in the transom and probably elsewhere, too.

But this catalog of woe is the lesser part of the story. *Nipinke* had an amiable disposition and always cooperated with her helmsman, however inexpert or inattentive. A roller furling jib and a boomed forestaysail meant only a few minutes to get her going whenever I felt like a casual spin, and she could be trimmed to sail herself much of the time. The engine was seldom used since she moved in the lightest airs and behaved predictably enough to be sailed up to docks and moorings no matter how crowded the harbor. I took *Nipinke* on innumerable day sails and weekend jaunts on Long Island Sound, on a cruise to Maine and back, and even raced her now and then, though it had been many years since she was competitive. Her deficiencies were such that I cannot suggest her in any sense as an ideal boat, but she gave me two years of fine service before

Bigger is not necessarily better,
but each step upward in boat size does
bring farther horizon within reach.
Sad to say, steps increase in length for
same degree of change. Counterclockwise
from lower left: 28-foot cutter Nipinke,
32-foot sloop Petrouchka, *54-foot*
yawl Tara, *and 40-foot sloop* Doubloon.

I sold her for exactly what I had paid.

Many owners of small cruising boats, no matter how pleased with their present craft, eventually begin to think of something larger. Sometimes this is the result of a careful analysis of specific requirements, but equally often it is a case of daydreams so vivid as to suggest a quite illusory substance. How many nights at sea are actually spent aboard yachts capable of an ocean crossing? Still, it really doesn't matter: the purpose of a sailboat is pleasure, and who is to say which gives more, the contemplation of a Bermuda Race or a passage to Tahiti in one's own boat, or the fulfillment?

In my own case, I had the presence of three children to support the idea of a more substantial boat as soon as my bank balance would permit. (This was not the main reason, of course, but it sounded good.) I was credulous enough, as so many novices are, to fall for the concept of the cruiser-racer, that chimera so beloved of the ex-soap salesmen who write boat ads. *Petrouchka* was only thirty-two feet overall, but her 10-foot beam gave her an enormous interior. Her light displacement, fin keel, and broad beam made her more like an overgrown dinghy than anything else, and like a dinghy she had to be kept light and sailed on her bottom.

Petrouchka was capable of astonishing speed when properly handled, and we were quite happy with her racing performance. But I really wanted her for long-distance cruising, and I hoped her speed would compensate for her relatively small size for this purpose. As a cruising boat she was a flop. With her capacious lockers full she was sluggish under way. At sea she lurched drunkenly about. Not for a moment could the tiller be let go, and when she heeled it sometimes took two people to control her. To keep her on my side meant changing jibs and rolling reefs in and out of the main.

We raced *Petrouchka* a lot, which was fun, but her deficiencies as a serious cruiser became all too evident when we sailed her to the Bahamas and back to New York. I felt sad when I concluded that she was not for me, because she was a thoroughbred and it was not her fault I had been persuaded into a misalliance with her. A man from Chicago bought her, trucked her home,

A shower of spray is the champagne of the sailor. Small boat in a breeze of wind provides plenty for its crew. As these pictures show, sailing is for both sexes and for all ages—but not for all temperaments.

changed her name, and brought her in dead last in a Mackinac race. To change a boat's name brings bad luck.

Petrouchka was large enough to provide an adequate accommodation, including six berths, full headroom, an enclosed head, and a complete galley, plus a clear deck and sailing performance that was usually at least reasonable and often superlative. These virtues are common to nearly all modern boats over about thirty feet overall, many of which avoid the flaws that Petrouchka exhibited. Much of the versatility of smaller cruising boats is retained in the 30- to 40-foot range, with the addition of greater speed and space, beauty and strength.

Alas, the cost of a boat of a given type increases more or less as the cube of its length, and a jump from twenty-five to thirty-five feet overall may mean a tripling of the total investment needed. Pleasure cannot be quantified, but even so it is hard to believe a 35-foot boat offers three times as much as a 25-footer. The law of diminishing returns applies at sea as on land. Nevertheless, it is nice to make swift passages whatever the weather, and to have the room to cruise with the whole family or another couple for weeks at a time. To own a boat between thirty and forty feet overall is the goal of many sailors, and it is easy to appreciate why.

When I had concluded that Petrouchka had to be replaced, I had no clear idea of what I wanted to replace her with. My first thought was another boat somewhat like her only better adapted for serious cruising. But then I let my mind wander and briefly contemplated a catamaran or a trimaran, just then coming into fashion.

Except in the case of a centerboard dinghy, a monohull relies on ballast for most of its stability, on beam for the rest. A multihull depends entirely on its great beam to keep it upright despite the pressure of wind on its sails and the assault of waves on its hull. Without a third or a half of its displacement in the form of a lump of dead metal, a catamaran or trimaran needs less sail for a given cubic capacity and, by virtue of the reduced resistance its two or three appendageless hulls offer to passage through the water, such a craft is capable of higher speeds than a monohull of comparable size.

58-foot ketch Minots Light *twenty years
ago. Designed by John Alden and
built by Abeking & Rasmussen, each aided
by long experience with similar craft, even today
she comes close to being perfect cruising
boat.* Minots Light *is now painted
black and has been extensively modernized,
but her essential character is unchanged.*

Light and lively, a multihull is also much cheaper than its monohull counterpart.

But every advantage a multihull boasts seemed to me to be matched by a disadvantage. Multihulls are extremely sensitive to weight, and their performance drops sharply when overloaded—in contrast to the majority of monohulls, which are so heavy anyway due to their ballast that a few more people, a few more cases of beer make relatively little difference. Multihulls are very difficult to maneuver in close quarters and are virtually impossible to control under power in a cross wind. In order to save weight they are lightly constructed, and the knocking around at sea and in harbor that a monohull shrugs off as part of the game may jeopardize the integrity of a multihull.

On the whole, though, advantages and disadvantages tend to balance out, with one exception. To me, the crux of the matter lay in the one feature monohulls possess that is entirely absent from multihulls: ultimate stability.

Heel over a ballasted sailboat as far as you like, even turn it upside down, and if it is even moderately watertight it will always right itself. There is no point of no return. Do the same to a catamaran or trimaran and the outcome will be very different. Now there *is* a point of no return, a limit which, if exceeded, means a mess inshore, a likely tragedy offshore. Quite apart from the ones that break up, a certain number of responsibly designed, carefully built, and attentively sailed multihulls turn over every year—and stay over.

Each time a cat or tri enthusiast berates me for my fuddy-duddy preference for monohulls, I bring up the two catamaran capsizes I have actually witnessed. My interlocutor then pounces: "But tris are okay!" Are they? Even though I have not personally seen one turn over, I have seen photographs of inverted trimarans, and their greatest exponent, Arthur Piver, disappeared at sea in one of them. Perhaps he was struck by a ship or vanished deliberately to escape taxes, but perhaps not. I remain as unconvinced of the safety of multihulls at sea as I am convinced of the incomparable sport they provide in coastal waters with shelter and help not far away.

The question of another boat

40

From left: *Trimaran with
self-steering vane for long passages;
suitably serious start of overnight
race;* Duchess II *on sort of day
her crew dreams of in winter;*
Minots Light *tied to Finnish island
with anchor astern and
fire already lit in sauna ashore.*

was settled ten minutes after I learned that *Minots Light* was for sale. I had first seen her in Padanaram Harbor in Buzzards Bay. She lay in regal dignity at her mooring as I sailed past in *Nipinke,* yet there was a hint of unresolved tension about her, of barely concealed impatience to be outside in the chop of the bay. Her ketch rig testified to seriousness of purpose, her graceful lines proclaimed both swiftness and seaworthiness. I recognized *Minots Light* at once, though I had neither seen nor heard of her before: she was in almost every detail of form and rig precisely the boat I had always dreamed of having.

During a casual conversation with a broker at a City Island yard on a

November Sunday years later, I learned that *Minots Light* was laid up there for the winter and, furthermore, that she had just the previous day been put on the market. I borrowed a flashlight and went to the shed where she sat braced on her keel, a beached whale in the gloom. I climbed the rickety ladder and sat in her cockpit behind the wheel. My fingers gripped its dusty spokes. She heeled to the opulent wind that urged her forward under full sail. Puffy trade-wind clouds dotted the lambent sky, a pod of porpoises romped alongside, a pareu-clad girl picked a banana from the stalk tied to the shrouds. A smudge on the horizon was the atoll that was our destination, and that night at anchor in its lagoon we would sleep in hammocks slung

on deck, lulled by the murmur of surf on the white beach and the whisper of palm trees.

Minots Light is a 58-foot steel-hulled ketch that was designed by John Alden and built by Abeking and Rasmussen. I have now owned her for eleven years, and still shudder when I think of the prospective purchasers who turned up the day after I had made out a deposit check while still in the grip of my reverie.

By any objective analysis *Minots Light* is too large and too expensive to be a practical proposition. There is nothing I have done with her that could not have been accomplished in a boat displacing half or even a third of her thirty tons. Anyone following my example and going into hock for

four years to buy a boat whose annual bill for maintenance, insurance, and new equipment sometimes involves five figures is clearly a fool. But I am impenitent. I acquired *Minots Light* to fulfill a vision of a certain life style, not to please my accountant, and she has exceeded all my hopes. I can visualize other boats, quite different in a number of respects, that would serve my purposes just as well but not, I think, any better.

My family and I live aboard *Minots Light* an average of four months every summer, and we sail her anywhere we choose knowing she will get us there. Stores and personal gear for seven or eight people for a month disappear into her capacious lockers along with sails, three bikes, two rub-

43

ber dinghies and outboards, and a lot more. We can wait out bad weather without claustrophobia or running short of anything, and later can go fast enough under sail or power to make up lost time if necessary.

Most large sailboats need equally large crews. *Minots Light* does not, partly because she is rigged as a ketch and partly because pains have been taken to organize her efficiently on deck. With the help of the autopilot one person can cope with most tasks, and there is nothing, apart from handling the spinnaker, that requires more than two people in a pinch. Naturally things happen faster with more hands available, but they are not absolutely necessary.

But the main reason I am happy with *Minots Light* is less simply stated. What it amounts to is that I feel at home aboard her at sea and in port. Envy does not rot my soul when I look at other boats, however marked their superiority in one respect or another. I think it is always a mistake to choose a boat of any size on the strength of certain features only—speed, number of berths, number of rudders, or whatever—if elsewhere there is something unfriendly that mars the picture. It is no use having a boat that goes to windward like a witch if it skitters out of control on a run, or a boat that is a housewife's dream below if it looks like a potato and has the gait of a snail. And deficiencies that seem minor at first tend to swell into major ones in time: a helm that fights back, a cockpit with nothing to lean against, a flimsy mast always on the verge of collapse, berths only an acrobat can enter and only a midget can relax in. There are so many fine boats around that it is unnecessary to have one that does not come at least halfway toward establishing a bond of affection with its crew.

A few years ago, after three years of depredation by the sun, salt, and workmen of the Mediterranean, *Minots Light* needed a thorough overhaul. I also wanted to make some major alterations and install radar, new instruments, additional tankage, and so forth. A clear case of new wine in an old bottle, it would seem; surely a new boat would be a better investment? I looked into the matter carefully, and concluded that with just the right changes, each mandated by experience, plus a general face-lift, I would end up with exactly what I wanted, whereas there was always the risk that a replacement boat might be a lemon.

We sailed *Minots Light* from Île des Embiez in the south of France to her builder's yard in Germany. As we motored up the Weser River toward Lemwerder, I wondered whether the craftsmanship so evident around me on board was still alive at Abeking and Rasmussen. When we got there, a walk through the yard showed that, if anything, the prevailing standards of skill and artistry were higher than they had been seventeen years earlier. It was hard to stick to my resolve to upgrade *Minots Light* in place of having a new vessel faultlessly shaped of aluminum and stainless steel and teak.

During the winter *Minots Light* was virtually taken apart and reassembled with new replacing old wherever there was any advantage in doing so. I can wish nothing better to any sailor than to have the experience of seeing his boat in such competent hands. Life is too short to cast aside an undepleted reservoir of happiness, and all too often a new boat means new problems, not new solutions.

When I first discussed what I wanted done with Horst Lehnert, the yard manager, and Harry Hartlieb, who was to supervise the project, I think they felt it was foolish to spend so much on a boat past her youth. At the end, they agreed with me that it had been the right thing to do. And every time that Hermann Schaedla, the yard's owner, and his wife come on board for a drink these days, I like to believe it is more than tact that leads her to plead with him to replace his own swift racing sloop *Indigo* with a vessel more like *Minots Light*.

Still, as time goes on, there are moments when I find myself envying the intimacy of boat, crew, wind, and water so evident when my children are off for a sail in their 15-foot sloop *Shenandoah*. Perhaps I should get another boat after all, smaller and better suited to casual, spur-of-the-moment ventures, or maybe I can persuade them to let me take *Shenandoah* to the secret places of the creeks and inlets that fringe the bay where *Minots Light* lies moored, to sample again the simple life on the water so hard to capture in a large vessel meant for more grandiose expeditions.

3/Ra

cing

Racing is the ultimate test of sailing skill. The aggregate results of a week of day races or of a season of overnighters will show unmistakably where the talent lies, but now and then a fluke will drop the champion to thirty-seventh while a stroke of inspiration elevates the novice to first. One plated ashtray and he is hooked for life. What is at first glance surprising is how many people continue to race even though they never make the prize list. Partly this comes about because hope springs eternal, but the main reason is that gaining a prize is only one of the many rewards that a race may bring its participants.

A race under sail, whether in hundred-dollar Optimist Prams for half a mile or in hundred-thousand-dollar ocean racers for three thousand, is an occasion of intense drama from well before the start until the final results are posted. Every detail involves a playlet of some sort. In the winter there is the discussion with the sailmaker about ordering new sails and modifying old ones. The yard is beseeched to bring the bottom to mirror smoothness. The rumor of an improved fitting means numberless phone calls and visits to chandlers. Tuning begins the moment the hull kisses the water and the mast is stepped. The trim of the hull, the tension of the shrouds, the leads of the sheets, nothing is inviolable in the quest for maximum speed. The crew is selected (or does the selecting; it is sometimes hard to tell which) and goes through its paces up to the warning gun of the first race of the season. Now the real testing begins.

The start is always exciting, more so than in any other type of contest. Dozens of boats mill around in apparent confusion, but at the five-minute gun they sort themselves out and at the start they hit the line with a precision that never fails to astonish. From then on, unless the wind fails, there is plenty to occupy mind and muscles. Sails are pulled in and let out a few millimeters at a time, mainsheet travelers are shifted a trifle, the halyard of the stretchy-luff genoa is tightened, loosened, tightened again. The helmsman watches the competing boats, keeps an eye out for a wind shift, and tries not

*Opening pages: Fresh
northwester sends fleet
of 30-foot Shields-class
sloops off to good
start on Long Island
Sound. These boats are
actively raced in several
U.S. yachting centers.*

to overstand the weather mark.

At the mark, spinnakers of every hue and pattern burst forth. A red-and-yellow hourglass provides a nice contrast to the more conventional nylon bubbles around it, though its owner does not seem to appreciate the compliments he receives. By the time the errant spinnaker has become mammiform like the rest, eight rivals have gone past, and the abashed crew works overtime at keeping it drawing well. No race is without some such incident to set it apart, to keep it alive in the memory.

At the finish—hours, days, or weeks later—the fleet straggles in. Even in a one-design race, there is a surprising spread between first and last boats. The great advantage of handicap competition is that the first boat to finish need not be the winner on corrected time, so no disgrace attaches to a late arrival—no immediate disgrace, anyway. It is always possible for a new wind to send in the tail-enders to cream the leaders. And equally possible for the wind to die, leaving the smaller boats adrift on an oleaginous sea while the crews of their swifter brethren celebrate ashore.

When the race is over, everybody is on an equal footing once more until the next time. After all, who knows which boat will suddenly sprout wings when its mainsail is recut, or be out of the running when the measurer buys a new tape?

One-design racing involves almost identical boats that compete on an even basis in each class. Few one-design boats have any living accommodations, since the races last only a few hours. But what hours they can be! It is a thrill even to watch a planing centerboarder, such as a Flying Dutchman, sizzle past, the crew out on a trapeze while the helmsman leans out as far as his stomach muscles permit. Planing is intoxicating and, once experienced, not easy to forgo. And the fact that it is hard, wet work, with brief inattention perhaps leading to a capsize, certainly to a lost place in the fleet, only adds to the fun.

Keel one-design boats are usually more stable and their crews need be less athletic. Not always much less, though. The Soling is a honey of a boat in almost every way, fast, nimble, and relatively cheap, but to sail it properly to windward means hanging

49

*Opposite: Spinnakers
have ways to avenge careless
handling. Left:* Oriana
*racing in Solent during Cowes
Week of 1971. Below:
Ghosting under spinnaker
calls for high
tolerance of frustration.*

51

Three closely matched sloops
approach windward
mark in Lipton Cup Race
off Miami. This race
is one of six held each winter
by Southern Ocean
Racing Conference in waters
of Florida and Bahamas.

over the rail and it is remarkably uncomfortable to do so for long.

The Flying Dutchman and the Soling are big-league boats, and considerable skill and dedication are needed to race them successfully. Hundreds of other one-design classes exist, one or another of which is likely to suit a given sailor in a given locality. It is pleasant to be able to set out for a race without the elaborate preparations needed on a larger craft, pleasant also to have uncomplicated ownership and maintenance with no risk of losing one's investment through obsolescence.

Many yachtsmen, myself included, feel sad at the passing from the active scene of the smaller meter-boats, the Sixes and Eights of the not-too-distant past. These lithe, elegant vessels were sheer delight to sail, and for half a century were actively raced in many parts of the world. Unfortunately they became expensive out of proportion to their size and speed, and, like the dinosaurs (some of which were also lithe and elegant), have been supplanted by wholly different species better adapted to the times. True, now and then a new Six is built for one

of the few contests still held for this class, and a fleet of ancient Eights still races in Scotland, but their battle for survival has been lost.

The Twelves, like their smaller sisters built to a formula so that they are very nearly, but not quite, alike, are still alive thanks to the triennial America's Cup competition. It is great sport to sail on a boat on which no concessions whatever have been made to human or financial frailty, and no experience in today's yachting can compare with participating in a match race in Twelves. I have had the good fortune to race in both a Six and a Twelve, in the former as skipper (we won) and in the latter as a member of the foredeck crew (we lost); no other type of sailboat has since been able to satisfy me in quite the same way.

Handicap racing usually means larger boats and more extended courses than one-design racing. There is more opportunity for experimentation, more variety in the problems that arise. An element of passage-making is involved in overnight and longer races; the skills of the navigator, the meteorologist, and the cook are needed on board,

*Racing stretches people
and boats to limit. Top: Sail
is shortened in heavy
weather to keep speed high,
not to increase comfort.
Above: Tension is high at
marks of course. Right:
Tempest is new Olympic class.*

54

and not infrequently those of the carpenter, the electrician, and the plumber as well. Organizing an entry for a major race can take a year or more of effort—all of it as rewarding in its own way as the race itself, perhaps even more.

Even the humblest local overnight race has an aura of high adventure about it. Luck as well as skill is involved, since a quirk of the weather may shift the odds in a flagrantly unfair way. This adds to the fun, or at least to the fun of those who suspect that, were the best man always to win, they never would.

I owe my first racing success to a cold front. The start of the race was to be in Little Neck Bay in the early evening. The club launch took us out to *Petrouchka* at her mooring off City Island an hour and a half before. Dick, Jim, and Are got things organized on deck as I reviewed the course and our strategy. Germaine made sandwiches and soup, which we ate hastily. Then the mainsail went up, the pennant was cast off, and we sailed slowly through the fleet of moored boats. In clear water the genoa was hoisted for the reach south to Kings Point.

Two dozen boats were already near the starting line when we arrived. Some were timing their runs to the line, others were practicing tacking and sail changing in a last-minute drive for perfection. Most boats were just sailing around casually, their crews exchanging ribald shouts. Nearly all were familiar from previous races, and I picked out a few hotshots to keep an eye on. The sky was clouding over, the wind a mild southwesterly. Based on past form I expected to finish somewhere in the middle of the fleet, behind experienced skippers who knew where to find every flicker of wind and swirl of current, ahead of those with slower craft than *Petrouchka* or with less keen crews.

The larger boats started first, their spinnakers blossoming against the indigo sky. I decided to start under the genoa and then get the spinnaker up immediately afterward; faint heart never won fair lady, but in the past we had lost through snarl-ups far more than we had gained through attempts at panache.

"Four minutes to go," Germaine said, stopwatch in hand. The end of the line near the committee boat had been

Preceding pages: Shields-class
sloops in close quarters. Good racing
crews are fast and precise in
their work; talent helps but practice is
indispensable. Helmsman must
be expert on racing rules and
able to think quickly
in situations like that opposite.

preferred by the big boats, but its advantage seemed to me too small in a seventy-mile race to be worth fighting for a good place there. I headed for the buoy marking the other end of the line. "Three minutes." We tacked and began to reach away from the line. "Two minutes." It was obvious that again the bulk of the fleet would start near the committee boat, so we would be all right at the middle of the line. "One minute forty seconds." We jibed and headed back. Dick and Are got the pole in place and checked that the spinnaker halyard and sheet were clear. "Twenty seconds." Refugees from the crush near the committee boat were all around us, but we were still in the clear. "Ten seconds." Some bastard was on our windward quarter taking our wind, and it looked as though we would be late. "Now." The starting gun went off. We were two boat lengths short. Not too good, but not too bad, either.

Dick hoisted the spinnaker, then dropped the genoa as Jim gathered it in. Are and Germaine trimmed the spinnaker and the needle of the Little Captain speed log crept up past six knots. I looked around. Three boats in our division were well ahead of us, the rest either approximately level or in back of *Petrouchka.*

We maintained our relative position in the fleet as we rounded Kings Point and made for Execution Rocks. It was fine sailing, and everybody relaxed after the tension of the start. "Look behind you," said Jim. I turned and saw a yellow sky where the sun was setting. Yellow, not golden. Soon a long black cloud obscured the horizon, as if a reflection of our black spinnaker.

By the time we were past Execution the cloud filled nearly half the sky, a dreadful sight, evidently the grandfather of all line squalls. One by one the other boats took in their spinnakers, and every foredeck had a pair of figures busy hanking on a storm jib. The wind was still no more than twenty knots, but that cloud was ominous.

Petrouchka was strongly built and strongly rigged, new that spring but well shaken down, and I decided to leave the spinnaker up as long as the wind stayed behind the beam. Nowadays full-size spinnakers are always kept flying in a race even when the wind is past gale force, but in the fifties this was still uncommon. Or uncom-

60

Duel between similar boats
is exciting event that brings
out best in all hands.
Left: Figaro *and* Bay Bea
in offshore race. Below:
Match race between 12-meters
Heritage *(foreground)*
and Intrepid. *Bottom: Two*
Solings *meet. Problem*
in racing is to maintain top
performance even when
competing boats are not nearby.

Spinnakers flying, weekend
racers reach finish
line marked by committee boat.
Winner is usually boat
that makes fewest mistakes.
Brief fumble in changing sail
is enough to separate
winner from runner-up.

mon that night, anyway. As the squall struck it felt as though a giant hand had seized the transom and was shoving us forward might- ily. *Petrouchka* was doing over eight knots, remarkable for a 32-footer, and we were filled with equal measures of joy and terror. The others thought I knew what I was doing; I kept the truth to myself.

Finally, as the whine of the rig- ging reached a crescendo, a gust struck from forward of the beam and *Petrouchka* swung around and lay over on her starboard side un- til the spinnaker was in the water and the cockpit coaming was submerged. The knock- down could not have taken more than a few seconds to happen, but it seemed agonizingly

slow. None of us had undergone a knockdown in such a large boat before, and we simply hung on unbelievingly as water sloshed into the cockpit. With a great flapping of the sails *Petrouchka* rose from her undignified posi- tion and off we roared once more into the darkness. Still stunned, we did not at first realize that the fall of the spinnaker halyard had gone adrift and was trailing behind us in the water.

When we had recovered our wits we pumped the bilge dry, dumped the water out of our seaboots, and retrieved the halyard fall. The wind was easing, though still robust, and behind us we could see spreader lights going on and spinnakers be- ing reset. An hour later Germaine spotted the buoy off the Connecticut shore that was the turning mark of the course, and as we round- ed it I felt a twinge of regret as the spin- naker, still intact, was gathered in under the genoa. (The others felt only relief.)

Dawn saw us well on the way back, splitting tacks with the larger boats and smug as hell. I still recall with ignoble pleasure crossing the bow of the 44-foot yawl in which I had crewed in my first race the year before. The wind faded as we approached the finishing line, and for a dreadful moment vanished completely when we were still a few hundred feet away. But we eventually made it across, and despite my fears to the contrary the pewter pitcher I later received showed that the race committee had not absorbed too much beer to take our time correctly.

Today I no longer race because I find that a successful cruise yields me more pleasure than any race ever did. But my transition from apprentice sailor to journeyman—I do not claim to be a master sailor, though I hope to become one eventually—was accelerated by racing, and I had a lot of fun while learning a great deal in a short time.

In racing, people and yachts are pushed to their limits. Sometimes these limits are overstepped and mistakes are made, masts are lost. More often, valuable lessons are learned that more prudent sailing would never reveal.

I do not want to leave the impression that all races involve heroic events. Far from it. Calms are more often the enemy than gales. The point is that races do not wait upon the weather, and a season of racing is likely to yield more collisions with the elements than a season of cruising. And on a race one hundred percent efficiency is the goal all the time, whereas on a cruise the spirit of the occasion normally calls for less than that. Racing is the better teacher at the start of a sailing career; after that I am not so sure.

Nowadays I do my best to keep nature on my side. If this means I have to stay in a dreary harbor for days on end, so be it. I have wrung enough salt water out of my socks, as the saying so aptly goes, to feel no threat to my masculinity in relaxing warm and dry below while the masts shiver and rain sluices down. A valuable residue of my racing days is the knowledge that a well-found sailboat can take more of a beating than her crew can, and that the crew themselves can take more of a beating than they think. My cruising days testify to the proposition that one can sail widely and well and hardly ever take a beating. In cruising one stays away from the boundaries of prudence. But I don't think I would really know where those boundaries lie without having raced.

Race Week at

Block Island

In June of odd-numbered years, the Storm Trysail Club of Long Island Sound organizes a week of racing and related festivities at Block Island, off New England coast. In 1971, there were more than 250 boats, divided into seven classes, competing in the various events.

*Fog is common in Block Island
vicinity in June, and 1971 was no exception.
Several races had to be postponed
or canceled but, showing
traditional indifference to hardship of the sailor,
nobody seemed to mind very much.*

Race Week continued

*Four races finally were held;
in one of them only Class A survived time
limit. Combination of
fog patches and strong tides made life
interesting for navigators.
Winds were mostly light, but sturdy westerly
appeared for last race.*

71

4/Cru

Racing sailboats offer such a vivid spectacle that nobody notices the cruising boat go by them on passage to anywhere its skipper pleases. Not restricted by any handicap rule to an uncomfortable, hard-to-handle boat and not bound by any race committee to a particular course, the cruising man is free to do the kind of sailing he wants in the kind of boat he prefers. With two or four or six on board instead of eight or ten or twelve, the good life can be lived by all hands as enchantment replaces struggle as the theme of the venture.

Cruising is to sailing as feasting is to eating. More of everything is available, it is all of the very best, and variety and surprise add sparkle to the occasion. A feast is more expensive than a meal and takes longer to prepare, but the rewards are in proportion. Although racing and day sailing have honorable places in the diet of the sailor, they are apt to pall after a while, and a well-planned and well-executed cruise provides a chance to gorge on the food of the gods.

What is cruising under sail like? To me it offers a feeling of freedom I have never experienced on land. With the boat fully stocked with food, water, and fuel, only time limits where I can go. If I feel like crowding on sail to take full advantage of a fair wind, I do so; if I want to anchor in some pretty cove for a swim, lunch, and a siesta, I do so; and if I think it sensible to turn on the engine to get to shelter ahead of a threatening storm, why I do that, too. Of course, the feeling of freedom is an illusion, nobody can be truly free anywhere, but illusion is the staff of life and this one is better than most.

Cruising offers boundless opportunities to exercise the sailor's skills in a noncompetitive atmosphere. The cruising men I know approach their tasks in no less a spirit of perfectionism than my racing friends, but their goals are quite different. Every boat is a winner on a cruise, so it really is the game itself that matters, not who comes in ahead of whom. There are times when it is more rewarding to sail slowly than to sail fast, and places where the long way round, not the most direct course, is the right route. It is the skipper's prerogative to decide where to go and how on a cruise, not that of a committee meeting months earlier.

Cruising does not necessarily mean a new destination every year. Some regions are so satisfying to a particular temperament that repeated visits only enhance their appeal. For instance, the Baltic Sea, like the coast of Maine, has a lien on my soul that strengthens with the passage of time. I have enjoyed fine cruises elsewhere, yet there is something about the harmony of sea, land, and sky in Maine that drew me there year after year when I lived in New York, and something about the harmony of the same elements in the Baltic that draws me there year after year now that I live in Europe.

Other sailors have other preferences. Hundreds of cruising boats regularly return to such waters as those of southern New England, Chesapeake Bay, Georgian Bay and North Channel in the Great Lakes, and the vicinity of Vancouver Island in the Pacific Northwest, and, farther afield, to the West Indies and the Mediterranean as well. A few of my cruising friends cannot bear to go to the same place twice and are driven by their personal demons to remote corners of the world. More of them eventually find what they want somewhere and then take pleasure in repeating certain passages and revisiting certain harbors and anchorages, each time finding a fresh delight.

The critical element in a successful cruise is an exact match between resources and project. The basic determinants are the boat and the available time, the variables are the crew and the itinerary. Satisfying cruises have been made in 14-foot dinghies, and even a weekend may not be too brief with luck in the weather. A larger boat and more time offer more scope, provided their advantages are not canceled out by too large a crew and too rigid a plan.

For a coastwise cruise in waters in which shelter is handy, a crew of two is enough on even a large boat if its gear is properly arranged. My wife and I have often cruised by ourselves on *Minots Light* for periods of up to several weeks. Four people, if they are the right ones, is better when something ambitious is in prospect, but six may be crowding things unless three separate cabins are available. With more than six, the rat effect takes over: past a certain critical

75

*Every cruise in Maine can be voyage of
discovery, since no lifetime is long
enough to visit all its coves and islands.
This 40-foot yawl is ideal for
exploring Maine coast, small enough
to poke into snug anchorages yet large
enough to be self-sufficient
when fogbound in remote harbors.*

density, rats in a cage go berserk.

Alas, some cruises turn out to be disasters, almost invariably because of guest trouble. On a race, the common purpose overrides personal considerations, and there is always plenty for everyone to do. On a cruise, not every guest shares the skipper's temperament and personalities grate all too easily. The same person who grumbles at an early start is furious when his week is up and the boat is in the middle of nowhere with no simple way for him to get home. A man accustomed to a drink or three at lunchtime will not be pleased when the skipper locks up the bottle until nightfall. Seldom will two women get along if this is their first time together in close quarters.

But with the right people on board it is another story. Every spring Karen and Are spend ten days on *Minots Light* with us while all our children are still in school, and I can imagine no nicer way to start the season. We are accustomed to one another and to the boat, everybody knows what he or she is supposed to do, and the occasional squall or miserable harbor is taken in stride. Are is a fire-eater, ever willing to handle sail the better to brush away the stale traces of winter. Karen has an eye for shape and color, and delights in the constant metamorphosis of our surroundings. The four of us spur one another to look anew at the sailor's world and find fresh treasures in its compass.

The members of a cruising party need not all be experienced sailors, although it is tempting fate to take sedentary people unaccustomed to the disciplines of expeditionary living. One summer two old friends who had never sailed before joined us for a passage from Helsinki to Stockholm. The weather was dreadful. Yet Bibi and Leon, dead game, stayed on deck through the worst of it day after day to crank winches, furl sails, and otherwise make themselves useful. Their reward came in a sauna on a little island along the way when Leon pushed the temperature past 240 degrees Fahrenheit and I fled gasping to join the ladies in the cold Baltic as he laughed and laughed.

In a race, a long thrash to windward is valued as a means of separating the men from the boys. On a cruise, who cares which is which? Give me a soldier's

77

Right: Typical scene in Long Island Sound. Dilemma of modern sailor is that knife in mast is cure for calms, but hard to accomplish with aluminum spar. Below: Lack of winds is seldom problem in waters around Mount Desert Island, Maine.

wind any time, a stout reaching breeze that sends the Harrier needle up to ten and our spirits to the sky.

Part of the planning for a cruise is to choose a strategy that maximizes fair winds and, if windward work is inevitable, that ensures it will take place in protected waters. For instance, it makes sense in a cruise Down East to make long passages, perhaps offshore, on the way there, with the prevailing southwesterlies all but guaranteeing a fast trip. Then, with plenty of time in hand, the return can be made at leisure, making use of the occasional brittle northwesterly and limiting any beating to stretches just long enough to remain fun.

The cruising sailor can also take advantage of canals and other inland waterways. A boat of suitable draft has many possible such routes open to it, some that offer convenient shortcuts, some that offer interesting journeys, a few that combine both attractions. Every spring and fall the Intracoastal Waterway that extends between Cape May and Key West carries swarms of yachts, few of whose owners would find the outside route in the Atlantic appealing.

A classic canal trip is the triangle cruise through upper New York State and part of Canada. A clockwise circuit means that the current in the St. Lawrence will be in one's favor. The Erie Canal is entered from the Hudson at Troy and followed through the Mohawk River Valley and Lake Oneida to Three River Point, from which the Oswego River takes one to Lake Ontario. Then the mast is restepped for a visit to the Thousand Islands and, later, Montreal. At Sorel in Quebec the mast must come down again as the canalized Richelieu River is followed to Lake Champlain and, from that lovely body of water, the Champlain Canal to rejoin the Hudson at Troy. The controlling depth is six and a half feet for this cruise, determined by the Richelieu locks. It is hard to think of a better way to spend a month afloat when salt water has temporarily lost its savor.

What characterizes cruising is not living on board a yacht—plenty of cruises are made in day sailers whose crews sleep ashore in tents—but that home waters are left behind. To the enduring fascination of sailing itself is added the appeal of visiting an un-

*Thousands of boats head south
each winter in search of sun's warmth.
Left: Comfortable ketch securely
moored in Withlacoochee
River near Florida's Gulf Coast.
Below: Gaff cutter enters
lock in misnamed Dismal
Swamp Canal of Inland Waterway.*

Below & bottom: Port Jefferson
on Long Island's north shore is magnet
for yachts on weekends during
summer. Right, from top: Cape Cod
anchorage; lighthouse in
Thousand Islands; Hadley Harbor
in Buzzards Bay. Far right:
Harbor scene anywhere.

82

83

familiar region with different land- and seascapes, perhaps also a different style of living from what one is accustomed to.

Eventually the cruising man will find no new destinations within easy reach and will begin to think about more distant places. Every year more and more American boats turn up in Europe, the West Indies, the South Pacific. Some of these craft are sailed over, others are shipped. It is common for a boat to be purchased in Europe and sailed there for a year or two before being brought home. Quite a number of Americans find foreign cruising so rewarding that they keep their boats abroad permanently and fly over each summer or other appropriate season.

Fortunately for Americans

*Cruising means lonely hours
at helm when mind drifts
and reality loses its substance.
Another boat is welcome
sight, especially when it is
fellow wanderer seduced
by artful sea to journey under
sail over its wide expanse.*

and Britons, in whose schools foreign languages are not taught as means of communication, English is closer to being a world language than any other. Charles V spoke Spanish to God, Italian to women, French to men, and German to his horse; such verbal dexterity, though good to have, is no longer necessary.

The universality of English was brought home to me in the pretty, fragrant cove of Banja on the island of Korčula in Yugoslavia. Just after we anchored there a few young people swam out to greet us. I spoke to them in halting German—no response. Germaine tried French—still no good. A friend on board essayed Italian—a blank. A long shot: *"¿Hablan Ustedes Español?"* Bewilderment. Finally one of them said

Extensive network of canals permits inland
passages across Europe. Below: French
lockkeeper's cottage; quay for transient
yachts in Paris. Bottom & right: Lock
near Dijon. Overhead clearance is limited, so
masts must be carried on deck. Canal
trip from Le Havre to Marseilles involves 165
to 232 locks, depending upon route.

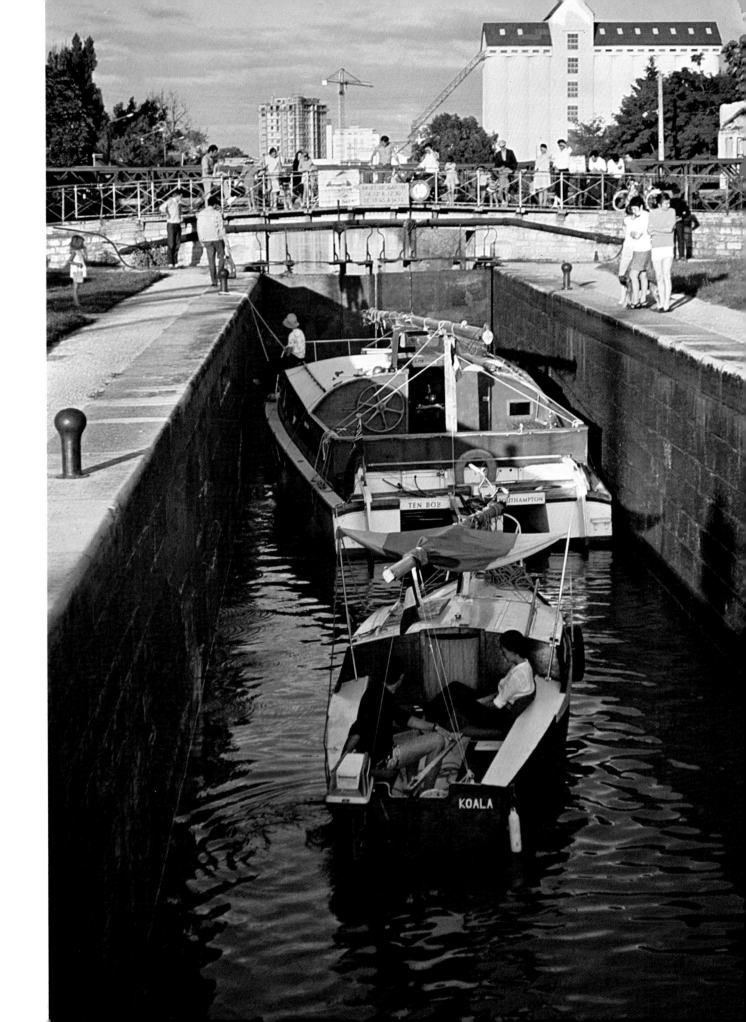

plaintively, "This is an American boat. Don't any of you speak English?"

But going foreign does mean learning words and phrases in other languages. The terminology of the sea has no less savor abroad than it has in English. Some terms bubble with intrigue: why is a mooring dolphin universally called a Duke of Alba in Europe? (Indeed, why is it called a dolphin in America?) I appreciate the sentiment behind calling a landlubber a land rat in Germany and a crab in Denmark, but why is he an elephant in France and a shoemaker in Spain? And even quite clear statements are not always to be taken literally. The Frenchman who shouts *"Je vous emmerde"* when you beat him to the last free berth in Saint-Tropez does not have quite that in mind, and when he goes on to speak of *"voile et vapeur"* it is you, not your auxiliary sailboat, that he refers to, and he does not mean what your dictionary tells you.

Nomenclature can present unexpected hazards. In England gasoline is called petrol, but in France *pétrole* is kerosene, which in England is paraffin. An English boy I once took as crew got a tank of kerosene instead of gasoline for the dinghy's outboard motor in Brittany, and spent a futile afternoon trying to get the motor to work properly.

Formalities can be a nuisance, but rarely more than that. A decade ago an awesome amount of red tape was required of a yacht in almost every European harbor, but nowadays official obtuseness seems to have found outlets elsewhere. Every year seems an improvement on the previous one. In 1963, for instance, *Minots Light* was boarded by customs officials not only in every Swedish harbor we stopped in (four separate batches of them on one day alone in Stockholm), but also in even the most remote anchorages, whereas in 1970 we saw only one customs officer during a three-week visit there. In 1964 we had to count every chocolate bar on board for Dutch customs (who on earth would try to smuggle chocolate *into* Holland?); in 1968 we were not once visited by them.

Sometimes customs officers come down to visit the yacht when it ties up, sometimes one must ask for them. Herman Melville was a customs inspector, but none of his modern counterparts seems to have more on his mind than a free beer. They are all obsessed with cigarettes and whiskey. Nobody on *Minots Light* smokes cigarettes, and since we prefer wine and beer there are seldom more than two or three bottles of spirits on board. This situation seems to amaze and upset customs men. However, after a ritual chat, some beer, and much polite smiling on both sides, eventually they go away. I have never had to give any official more than a beer or a shot of whiskey to get rid of him thus far, and in Italy, of all places, a harbor captain once even bought me a cup of coffee after issuing a *constituto* for the boat.

Europe is crisscrossed by an extensive network of rivers and canals that are as helpful to the cruising sailor as their counterparts in the United States. Thus a canal journey through France offers scenery to look at, places to visit, food to eat, and wine to drink that comprise a package hard to equal, while at the same time providing a safe way to cross Europe from north to south. The outside route from northern Europe to the Mediterranean means a considerable voyage in the open Atlantic, nothing special for a seaworthy yacht, but a long haul nevertheless.

The canals cut the distance from Le Havre to Marseilles from 1,876 miles to between 505 and 570 miles, depending upon the route.

A determined crew can make it from the English Channel to the Med through the canals in perhaps two weeks by leaving every day when the lockkeepers begin work at 0600 and not stopping until quitting time of 1930. To be in such a hurry is absurd, however. I remember one cold, rainy morning on the Marne in a chartered powerboat when we all felt in need of cheering up. We made fast under the bridge at La Ferté-sous-Jouarre and went for lunch to the Auberge de Condé for an absolutely perfect meal in every respect. The food and wine were excellent, the ambiance and service beyond reproach, and the bill came to a third what a comparable meal in Paris would cost. And I didn't even have to wear a tie. Afterward we took naps, and later a stroll through the town completed the occasion and brought us to nightfall. From one point of view, half a day wasted; from another, half a day well spent. Anyone who would pass over opportunities like this in favor of pressing on does not deserve the chance to make such a trip.

89

5/Wind

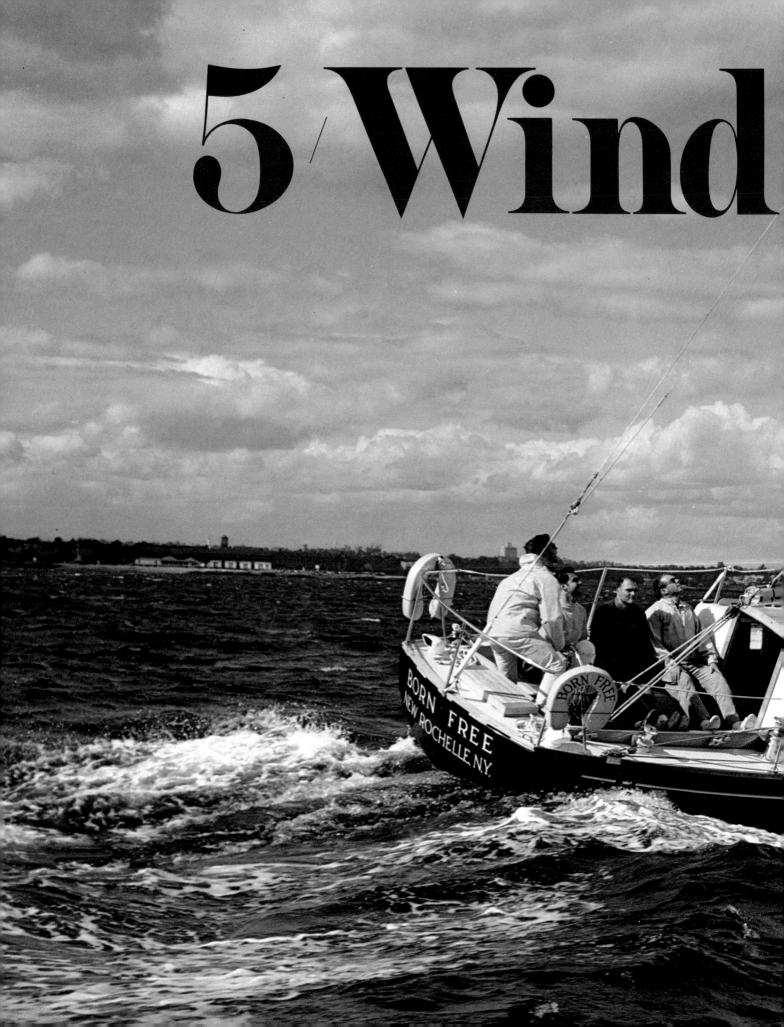

&Water

A sailboat floats on the sea and is driven by the wind. Wind and sea are the allies of the wise sailor, the antagonists of the foolish one. Though the elements will always have a certain insouciant unpredictability, their general patterns of behavior are well understood, and nobody has more reason to become acquainted with these patterns than the sailor.

The seas are not static bodies of water. Winds ruffle their surfaces into waves and drive great currents that profoundly influence climates around the world. And the twice-daily rise and fall of the tides is familiar to every coastal dweller.

Waves are produced by winds blowing over the surface of a body of water. When a wind starts to blow over a smooth water surface, ripples—the cat's paws of the sailor—begin to form whose crests are rounded and glassy in appearance. An increase in wind speed brings true waves with sharper crests; the stronger the wind, the longer it blows, and the greater the distance over which the wind has been in contact with the water, the higher the waves. These three factors govern the amount of energy transferred to the water and thus they govern the violence of the disturbance that results.

The relationship between winds at sea and the waves they cause is given in the accompanying table. In this table it is assumed that the wind has been blowing for enough time and over enough distance for the waves to attain their maximum height. For example, a 30-knot offshore wind produces waves typically 13½ feet high after blowing for ten hours or more over one hundred miles or more of open sea, but after three hours the typical wave height is only eight feet at this distance and ten miles offshore it remains four feet no matter how long a period of time is involved.

The term "typical wave height" is rather ambiguous, which is why different reference works quote different figures for the wave heights to be expected under specified wind conditions. And typical waves, however defined, are always considerably smaller than the giants that come along with enough regularity to make gales at sea such unpleasant affairs. In a given wind, waves half again higher than "typical" ones are unfortunately common, and still larger ones can be expected from time to time. Though a prolonged blow does not increase the typical wave height by much over the amounts given in the table, the likelihood of exceptional waves coming along does go up.

The table (page 94) shows the relationship of wind speed to the state of the sea surface in open water. The Beaufort scale is traditionally used by mariners to describe wind speed; it is named after Francis Beaufort, a British naval officer, who devised it in 1806. The virtue of this scale is that, with a little experience, winds at sea can be described in terms of it without an anemometer. Nowadays, with anemometers common, the Beaufort scale is less widely used than it formerly was, but many sailors still find it convenient and weather forecasts for shipping in many places still express winds in terms of the appropriate Beaufort number.

Winds are movements of air across the earth's surface. If we were somehow able to view the structure of the winds around the world, we would find three broad categories of motion. On the smallest scale are irregular eddies, no more than a few miles across, that are associated with such local phenomena as thunderstorms. Much larger are the enormous whorls, several hundred to a thousand or more miles across, that constitute the weather systems so conspicuous on weather maps. These weather systems may center about regions of low pressure, in which case they are called cyclones and exhibit counterclockwise winds in the northern hemisphere (clockwise in the southern), or they may center about regions of high pressure, in which case they are called anticyclones and exhibit clockwise winds in the northern hemisphere (counterclockwise in the southern). And, if we could somehow average out the winds of the large and small spinning air masses, we would discover vast systematic movements of air that make up the general circulation of the atmosphere.

The characteristic winds of three regions of the globe are important components of the general circulation of the atmosphere. Westerly winds predominate between 60°N and 30°N, in the equatorial belt from 30°N to 30°S easterly winds are

93

*Running under spinnaker
in big boat in robust wind
is experience without
equal. Considerable work
is needed to get best
from 72-foot yawl* Windigo
*going downwind, but
nobody grudges the effort.*

BEAUFORT SCALE

Beaufort number	Wind description	Wind speed, knots	Sea condition	Typical wave height, feet
0	Calm	Less than 1	Sea like a mirror	—
1	Light air	1-3	Ripples with scaly appearance, no foam crests	¼
2	Light breeze	4-6	Small wavelets whose crests have a glassy appearance and do not break	½
3	Gentle breeze	7-10	Large wavelets with crests beginning to break, perhaps scattered whitecaps	2
4	Moderate breeze	11-16	Small waves becoming longer, frequent whitecaps	3½
5	Fresh breeze	17-21	Moderate waves of greater length, many whitecaps and some spray	6
6	Strong breeze	22-27	Large waves begin to form, whitecaps everywhere, more spray	9½
7	Moderate gale	28-33	Sea heaps up and streaks of foam are blown from breaking waves	13½
8	Fresh gale	34-40	Moderately high waves of greater length, edges of crests break into spindrift, well-marked streaks of foam	18
9	Strong gale	41-47	High waves whose crests begin to topple over, dense streaks of foam, sea begins to roll	23
10	Whole gale	48-55	Very high waves with long overhanging crests, sea is white with foam and rolls heavily, visibility reduced	29
11	Storm	56-63	Exceptionally high waves, sea completely covered with foam, small- and medium-sized ships lost to view behind waves, visibility further reduced	37
12	Hurricane	More than 64	Sea completely white with driven spray, air filled with foam, visibility very poor	45

the rule, and between 30°S and 60°S they are again westerly. This is naturally a very simplified picture. The easterlies are weak near the equator itself and tend to come from the northeast in the northern hemisphere and from the southeast in the southern, for instance. But if we go up to an altitude of a mile or so above the ground, the air flow is much more regular and either directly east or directly west. Still higher up all winds are westerly whatever the latitude.

The various zones of regular wind were important to shipping in the days of sail, as their names indicate. Thus the steady easterlies on either side of the equator became known as the trade winds, while the region of light, erratic wind along the equator itself, where the principal movement of air is upward, constitutes the doldrums. The horse latitudes that separate the trade winds in either hemisphere from the prevailing westerlies of the middle latitudes are also regions of light winds and are supposed to have been given their name because of the practice of throwing overboard horses taken as cargo on vessels that were subsequently becalmed there and ran short of water.

Fair winds in the ocean also mean favorable currents. The friction of wind on water produces surface currents that parallel the major wind systems to a large extent. The northeast and southeast trade winds drive water before them westward along the equator to form the Equatorial Current. In the Atlantic Ocean this current runs head on into South America, in the Pacific into the East Indies. At each of these places the respective current divides into two parts, one flowing south and the other north. Moving away from the equator along the continental margins, these currents eventually come under the influence of the westerlies, which turn them eastward across the oceans. Thus gigantic whirlpools, known as gyres, are set up in both Atlantic and Pacific oceans on either side of the equator. Many minor complexities are produced in the four great gyres by islands, continental projections, and undersea mountains and valleys.

The western side of the North Atlantic gyre, a warm current that moves partly into the Gulf of Mexico and partly north along the American coast, is the familiar Gulf Stream. Forced away from the

*Fair winds and fair currents
are major help on long
passage; broad patterns are
shown on these maps.
Pilot charts give
detailed month-by-month
picture for each
of the world's oceans.*

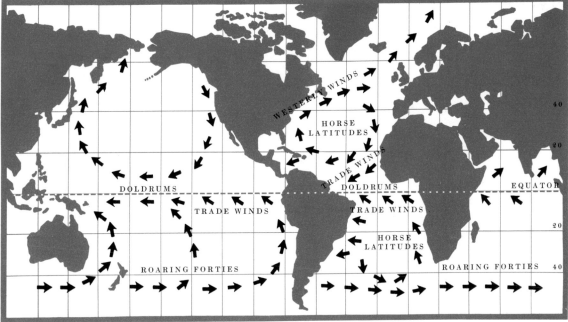

PREVAILING WINDS

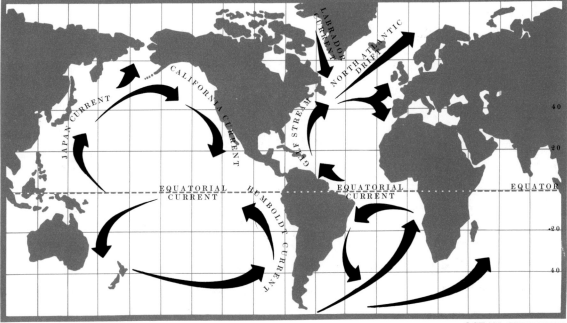

OCEAN CURRENTS

97

coast in the latitude of New Jersey by the prevailing westerly winds, this current moves northeastward across the Atlantic where it is called the North Atlantic Drift. On the European side of the ocean the Drift splits into one part that moves south to complete the gyre and another part that continues northeastward past Great Britain and Norway into the Arctic Ocean. To compensate for the addition of water to the polar sea, a cold current moves southward along the east coast of North America as far as New York; this is the Labrador Current. The North Pacific gyre forms the northward-flowing Japan Current along the coast of Asia, and the southward-flowing California Current along the west coast of North America.

The navigator of a sailboat must take ocean currents into account both in planning and in carrying out an offshore passage. In the narrow gap between Florida and the Bahamas the Gulf Stream may exceed four knots at times, and no sailor in those waters can ignore it. Elsewhere currents are usually less conspicuous but can still make a difference: a boat sailing from New York to the English Channel might with luck get an average boost of half a knot for the whole trip—perhaps 250 miles for free.

Special pilot charts issued by the Oceanographic Office of the Navy portray the average winds, currents, and climatic conditions for each ocean for each month. These are hypnotic documents, impossible to put down. To examine a set of them is to set forth on imaginary voyages with fair winds and fair currents all the way. And the more often the charts are studied, the more inevitable becomes the transition from imaginary voyages to actual ones.

Every time I look at the pilot charts for the North Atlantic, for instance, the plan of a year's circular tour assembles itself from the maze of colored lines and numbers that covers them. With dividers and calendar at hand the details fall into place.

The voyage begins in New York or Boston. From either of them to Scotland the course lies in the path of the prevailing westerlies, and late May or June is a good time to leave. Then comes a summer's exploration of northern Europe, starting with the west coast of Scotland and continuing to the Baltic via the Caledonian and

Göta canals to end in southern England in September. In the Bay of Biscay almost anything can be expected, but off the Iberian peninsula northerly winds are the rule and with any luck they can be carried down to Madeira and the Canaries. The steady draft of the northeast trades means a free ride to the West Indies in good time for Christmas in the sunshine and perfumed air of Grenada, or in the friendly atmosphere of Nelson's dockyard in Antigua. After a Caribbean winter the trades can be carried up to the Bahamas where southerly and then southwesterly winds take over for the final leg. As a bonus, a summer in Maine.

The pilot charts of the Pacific have more than one tempting circuit concealed in them. On more winter evenings than I can count, I have passed through the Panama Canal and continued on to the Galápagos and the remarkable wildlife that flourishes there. Then the southeast trades carried me to the Marquesas and through the dangerous but intriguing Tuamotus to renew my acquaintance with Tahiti, which has been going to hell for two hundred years yet is still a magic island. A flurry of red tape, a drink at Quinn's Bar, a drive to Point Venus to pay my respects to the memory of Captain Cook, and on to neighboring Moorea to anchor in Robinson's Cove. Still favored by the southeast trades, I saw myself going from Moorea to the other Society Islands, in particular Bora Bora, whose girls are the prettiest in the world, to the Cook Islands, and to the very aptly named Friendly Islands, which sour cartographers persist in referring to as Tonga. Then on to Samoa or perhaps Fiji for the hurricane season that lasts from December to April.

To complete the voyage I sailed south (with an occasional glance at the snow-covered trees outside my window) until a westerly component appeared in the wind, whereupon I headed east and then north to Tahiti and from there to Hawaii with the trades on the starboard beam. For fair winds the rest of the way I then had to go north past the North Pacific High, which gave me a fair current as additional compensation for the extra distance. As a final treat I went up to Alaska and down the Inside Passage along the Canadian coast to Puget Sound. Dreams like these are included at no additional

99

charge with every set of pilot charts.

Pilot charts, however, give only part of the story of the weather in the middle latitudes, which is more variable than anywhere else on earth. In the West Indies and Hawaii, both in the path of the northeast trades, one day follows another with hardly any change in temperature, humidity, or wind, whereas in nearly all parts of the continental United States and northern Europe abrupt changes in weather are commonplace. Although inconstant, middle-latitude weather is not random but is largely determined by the motions of warm and cold air masses and of storms derived from them through the belts of the westerlies.

An irregular boundary separates warm air in the westerly belts from the cold air of the polar regions. Great tongues of cold air at times sweep down over North America, and at other times warm air from the tropics extends far northward. The cold air is eventually warmed and the warm air cooled, but a large body of air can maintain more or less its original temperature and humidity for days or even weeks. These tongues of air, or isolated bodies of them that become detached, are the air masses of meteorology. The kind of air in an air mass depends on its source: a mass from northern Canada is cold and dry, one from the North Atlantic or North Pacific is cold and humid, one from the Gulf of Mexico is warm and humid, and so forth.

The contact zone between a warm and a cold air mass is inevitably a disturbed region. In general, the lighter air of the warm mass rides up over the heavy air of the cold one, so the contact surface is inclined. The line where this so-called frontal surface meets the ground is known as a front. As the air masses move in an easterly direction with the drift of the prevailing westerlies, the frontal surfaces at their margins move with them. A front with a cold mass to the west and a warm mass to the east is a cold front; a front that separates warm air on the west from cold air on the east is a warm front. The progress of a cold front brings cold air in place of warm, and the progress of a warm front brings warm air in place of cold.

As warm air rises along an inclined frontal surface it is cooled and part of the moisture it contains condenses out. Ac-

Blustery sky means chance of squalls. In unsettled weather racing prizes go to best forecaster of wind shifts. But afterwards there may be hard slog going home.

cordingly clouds and rain are usually associated with both kinds of front. A cold frontal surface is generally steeper than a warm one, since cold air is burrowing under warm air along the surface, and the temperature difference is greater, so rainfall on a cold front is heavier but briefer than on a warm front. A cold front with a large temperature difference is often marked by violent thunder-squalls and sometimes even tornadoes.

The first sign of an approaching warm front is the appearance of wispy cirrus clouds—mare's-tails—at high altitude. These clouds are at the upper edge of the warm air mass and are five hundred to a thousand miles ahead of the warm front itself. Next an opalescent film of cirrostratus fills the sky, and a few hours later streaks of gray altostratus gradually blot out the sun. All this time the pressure has been falling and the wind has been backing (swinging counterclockwise from its original direction, that is, N→W→S→E→N). Finally, a day or two after the cirrus first came into view, thick banks of nimbostratus darken the sky and a steady rain begins to fall. The wind increases somewhat and gusts may occur as the front itself passes. The temperature rises, the wind veers (swings clockwise from its original direction, that is, N→E→S→W→N), and the pressure soon steadies. After a while the rain tapers off into drizzle and stops, but the air remains muggy. Low clouds may persist, and visibility may be poor for some time afterward.

A cold front arrives with more drama. The intruding mass of cold air forces the warm, moist air before it upward to produce a heavy bank of dense cumulonimbus. A strong cold front appears as a squall line arriving from the west or northwest, an ominous black streak from horizon to horizon. As it passes by, the temperature falls rapidly, rain pours down, and the wind veers sharply from southwest to northwest in a succession of vicious gusts. Rumbles of thunder, perhaps a shower of hail further enliven the proceedings. The wind speed may jump ten or fifteen knots in less than a minute in the gusts, a possibility not to be taken lightly by the sailor. Finally, half an hour later, the squall line is well to the east and the sky begins to clear. The air is now cool, dry, and bracing, visibility is excellent, and a vigorous northwesterly

*Sky often hints of weather to come.
Clockwise from above: Fast-moving mare's-tails
mean wind will back and increase later;
perhaps calm before storm, more likely little
change in prospect; time to hank on
smaller jib and check reefing gear; "red
sky at night, sailor's delight";
"red sky in morning, sailors take warning."*

settles down to blow for a few days. A grand wind for a fast passage south.

Weather changes in the middle latitudes are usually associated with the passages of fronts; hence the traditional rhymes of the mariner. "Red sky at night, sailor's delight" makes sense because the sun sets in the west, and if it is able to illuminate nearby clouds with its red twilight rays, the sky must be clear past the western horizon. Fronts come from the west, so no frontal passage is imminent. The sun rises in the east, and if the sky is red at dawn, it must be clear to the east but filling with cloud from the west. "Red sky in morning, sailors take warning" thus portends the arrival of a warm front.

Many regions are regularly visited by local winds whose extent is miles or dozens of miles, not the hundreds or thousands of miles characteristic of weather systems. Familiar to every sailor is the sea breeze that is his salvation on a quiet summer day. At daybreak all is calm, the sky clear. As the morning wears on the land warms up, since the heat absorbed from the sun's radiation stays at the surface. The temperature of the sea hardly changes, however, since incoming solar energy is shared throughout a thicker volume of water. The air over the warm land rises, and cooler, denser air from the sea—the sea breeze—sweeps in to replace it. (The complete picture is more complicated, but not very different in its essence.) By noon, with any luck, a steady 10-knot wind will be blowing toward the shore, increasing in strength in the later afternoon. The sea breeze is limited to a band a dozen miles or so wide parallel to the coast, but in that band it offers fine sailing. Then in the evening the land cools rapidly while the sea stays at a constant temperature, and the sea breeze dies away. A total calm may ensue.

Later a land breeze may start, with cool air from the shore moving out over the now-warmer sea. When the coast is hilly, cold night air sinks down the slopes and flows across the water because it has nowhere else to go; the result is called a katabatic wind to distinguish it from the true land breeze that arises from the difference in surface temperature between land and sea. Such offshore winds are seldom robust and begin a few hours after sunset, say around midnight, if the sky is clear or partly cloudy. By dawn all is calm once more. If there is a substantial amount of cloud, the cooling of the land is retarded and there will be no offshore wind.

The blasting winds and crashing seas of an ocean gale are strangers to most lakes, rivers, and bays. Instead, local sailors must contend with quirks of wind behavior that provide delight and despair in equal measure. The contours of the land are now as significant as the pressure contours on a weather map. A hilly coast to windward means patches of gust and calm as the airstream is channeled through dips in the landscape; close to shore, even houses and groves of trees have the same effect. The fastest course between two points in an inland lake is seldom a straight line in a diffident summer breeze.

Another familiar habit of winds is to follow the channel of a river with steep banks. To make progress upstream against a head wind means hugging the inner side of a bend here to get a lift from an eddy in the current, swinging out into the middle there to avoid being blanketed by high ground. A knack at puzzle-solving is as useful as sailing skill itself in such conditions.

The purpose of sails is to coax from the wind a portion of its energy to power the forward motion of the boat. Which sails are best for a particular boat depends upon the strength of the wind and its direction relative to the heading of the boat. Beating to windward—where suction on the lee sides of the sails does the work—is different in the aerodynamic principles involved from running downwind, and what serves for ghosting in a phantom breeze on a certain point of sailing will need drastic revision when the grandfather of that breeze comes booming along.

Because no sailboat can go directly into the wind's eye but must tack back and forth across it, a disproportionate amount of time tends to be spent in sailing to windward. Hence windward ability comes first in the design of most rigs, whether for racing, day sailing, or coastwise cruising; it is easy to forgive a close-winded boat any imperfections in other departments. Few sights infuriate the sailor more than that of another vessel blandly eating to windward of him, and a squall somersaulting over the water may mean serious trouble for a boat that cannot point high.

*New IOR rating rule encourages closely
similar racing boats with sloop rigs
and fin keels. Result is fine performance
with strong crews in deep water, as
Improbable shows (opposite), but most boats
built to rule are less suitable for
cruising than formerly. Who benefits from
situation is mystery to many yachtsmen.*

Modern hulls, rigs, sails, and winches are so efficient and (usually) reliable that windward ability can normally be taken for granted. Oddly enough, it is the ironically named "free wind" that nowadays presents difficulties, a complete reversal of the situation when gaff rig was standard. Going downwind is not at all as simple as it appears in the abstract if spirited performance is required. Though all sailors face the same difficulties in this regard, they are especially relevant to the deepwater sailor since nearly all ocean passages, whether racing or cruising, are made with fair winds.

There are two chief problems here. The most basic is that, in going downwind, the boat's speed subtracts from the wind speed, whereas on other points of sailing the boat's speed adds to the wind speed. In the same conditions, going downwind means less apparent wind for propulsion. Because the pressure the apparent wind exerts is proportional to the square of its speed, a given area of sail in a given true wind will be much less effective downwind than on any other heading. An apparent wind of thirteen knots on a beat may well shrink to five knots on a run, a reduction of 62 percent in speed and of 85 percent in pressure. Actually, because the same sail behaves differently on different headings, the change in applied force will not be exactly 85 percent, but it will be plenty in any case. The second problem is that downwind the sails forward tend to be blanketed by the sails aft. Hence there is not only less pressure available, but less sail area for it to act upon.

A spinnaker is a huge bag of filmy nylon that solves the problem of less apparent wind by its great area and the problem of blanketing by being propped out to windward by a pole. When all goes well, the spinnaker affords more pleasure than any other sail. When something goes wrong with it, it usually goes *very* wrong, sometimes spectacularly so.

What makes a spinnaker both so exciting and so wayward is that it is firmly attached to the boat only at its top. The cat's cradle of lines on the pole is never enough to produce a wholly secure anchorage for the windward clew of the sail, and the sheet on the leeward clew is so long that only minimal control is possible. A flick of the wind or a

*Fine going, but now is time to plan
tactics and strategy in case wind grows
stronger. Force of wind increases
with square of its speed, and routine
tasks soon become hard to carry
out when weather deteriorates. Big boats
offer good working platforms, but
huge sails can be problem in real blow.*

moment's inattention at the helm and the spinnaker may twist savagely or cause a sheer to windward that ends in a knockdown.

A racing boat must carry a spinnaker—more likely several—and all the gear associated with it: there is no alternative. On a small cruising boat, two on deck can set, trim, and hand a spinnaker, and since the basic speed of such a boat is low to begin with, a spinnaker makes sense. On a larger cruising boat, it would seem to be missing the point to take several extra people along on a cruise just to tend this one sail. The real question in trying to assure adequate downwind performance in a cruising yacht of any size is not how to arrange efficient spinnaker gear, but how to replace the spinnaker with sails that are safer and easier to handle.

What are the alternatives to carrying a spinnaker? The simplest is to tack downwind with reaching sails, counting on the greater speed of broad reaching to compensate for the zigzag path needed. Here is a table of the extra distance Δ sailed in going from one point to another dead downwind of it, while making tacks at the angle θ relative to the direct path.

θ	Δ	θ	Δ
0	0 %	25°	10%
5°	0.4%	30°	15%
10°	1.5%	35°	22%
15°	3.5%	40°	31%
20°	6.4%	45°	41%

Tacking downwind is profitable if the increase in boat speed exceeds the increase in distance. Generally, the lighter the wind, the more it pays to bear away. Almost always a deviation of 20° or 25° yields a substantial dividend if a spinnaker is not carried. In strong winds there is less to be gained, and jibing is harder as well.

When a spinnaker is not taken, a special reaching jib can be a good investment. Such a jib should be as large as possible, but not as light as possible since it is nice to be able to use it to windward in light airs. On some headings it is an advantage to sheet a reacher via a block at the end of the main boom, but its clew has to be at the right height to avoid an undue twist in the sail.

One of the virtues of ketches and yawls is that they can set mizzen staysails. Docile under all circumstances, a mizzen staysail can provide a worthwhile push

when the wind is just right. Experienced cruising men do a lot more reaching than racing men, because they try to avoid beating to windward and tack downwind instead of running under spinnaker. Hence a mizzen staysail will be used more often on a cruising boat than on a racing boat, and the sneers of the hotshots about the limited usefulness of this sail can be disregarded.

Reaching in a seaway, a jib and mizzen staysail combination means no booms to worry about while there can be plenty of area that is easy to cope with. This rig is especially valuable when a gale is dying out, leaving a vicious sea but not quite enough wind to hold the ship steady.

Not always is tacking downwind possible, of course. In such an event a reaching jib can be held out to windward by a spinnaker pole, which is easy to do on a small or moderate-size boat. On a large boat this is a major project, however. The first time I tried to set the reacher on *Minots Light* with a spinnaker pole to its clew, the damn thing wrapped six times around the headstay. No spinnaker ever wrapped tighter than that sail. We were four on deck, which was enough, the true wind was fifteen knots, which was not too much, all the gear was in good shape . . . but it happened, and we spent an anxious half hour clearing the sail. It eventually turned out to be a superb arrangement—I am sure a spinnaker would not have given more than a fraction of a knot more speed but would have needed much more tending. However, I resolved to do without the pole in the future, not just because of the wrap but because the pole is twenty feet long and needs two men to deal with it.

What I finally settled on was something I have never seen done elsewhere: the reacher is sheeted to the end of the *mizzen* boom when going dead downwind. Perhaps this scheme is an old dodge fallen into disuse, but if not I am delighted to have had the privilege of making a contribution to sailing, even if it turns out that it only works on *Minots Light* and next year she loses her mizzenmast because of the considerable thrust developed at the gooseneck.

The procedure is straightforward and easy to accomplish. A snatch block is made fast to the end of the mizzen-staysail sheet, which passes through a block at the end of the mizzen boom and is always in place. The snatch block is snapped on the jib sheet and winched out to the boom end while the jib sheet is eased accordingly. The mizzen boom is all the way out, of course. The main-sail is out on the other side of the boat. Although my reacher was not designed for this purpose, its clew is at the right height because it was intended to be sheeted to the end of the main boom. What is remarkable about this rig on *Minots Light* is that it is stable and effective when the wind is up to about 20° on either side of dead aft. And it is a simple matter for one person to pull the reacher out to the mizzen-boom end, or to free it to function in the usual way. There seems to be a slight gain in speed when the mizzen itself is up, too, but the prime movers are the main and the reacher.

Possibly only a ketch can sheet a reacher to the mizzen boom profitably; the mizzen of the average yawl is so small that the jib would most likely be hooked inboard excessively. A good deal depends on the sail in question and just where the skipper draws the line between convenience and efficiency. But it is such a handy arrangement that it is worth an experiment on any two-master.

Most cruising boats which set out on long trade-wind passages are fitted with special running sails to capitalize upon the steady winds from astern that can be expected. Over the years a variety of schemes has been tried, but only one seems to have become widely accepted.

In the preferred method a pair of large, high-clewed jibs of light cloth are used, one on each side. The clews are held out by booms hinged to the mast high enough off the deck so that, when not in use, the outer ends of the booms come down to the shrouds on either side of the mast and are secured there above the lifelines. The booms are best made from aluminum; they need not be especially heavy or large in diameter since they undergo only moderate compressive stresses and not the kind of punishment a spinnaker pole gets when it is forced against the headstay on a close reach. No topping lifts or foreguys are required. The outer end of each boom is made fast to the clew of its sail and goes up and down with the sail when it is hoisted and taken down.

The running sails themselves are usually hanked to two special stays of fairly light wire from the masthead to fittings a few feet apart on deck up forward. Each stay should be just the right length to permit it plus its turnbuckle to be made fast to the tang of the forward shroud on its side of the ship. Then, when idle, the stay can be set up with the turnbuckle and will be out of the way for normal sailing. A short wire span will be needed to extend the stay to the proper length when it is to be employed.

There is no reason why both running sails have to be identical. For instance, one of them can be made from cloth heavy enough to be used as a conventional jib topsail in light and moderate airs, with the other much lighter sail meant for running only.

The central problem—better, the central pleasure—of sailing is to make the most of whatever wind one finds. There are no standard solutions that hold for all boats and all crews in a given wind, and every sailor must make his own decisions on the basis of his experience and judgment. Things are never exactly the same twice. And just when the right sails are up and trimmed perfectly, the wind inevitably shifts or the course must be altered, which means reassessing the situation and taking new action. A discouraging prospect? Few sailors would have it any other way.

111

rms

Gale. A mild word, silken, a girl's name in other spelling. A poor choice to describe the screaming wind that inflames the sea into cusps of white-flecked, malevolent fury. To be caught out at sea in a gale is an indelible experience. And a valuable one, for the lessons thus learned are not likely to be forgotten. The single most important lesson is that you can't fool a gale. You can regularly kid the boys at the bar, the measurer, the race committee, your crew, your wife, yourself, but when the wind begins to whistle and the sky to turn a mottled angry gray, kidding doesn't work any more. Every weakness of the boat will be rudely exposed, every weakness of the skipper relentlessly punished.

By weaknesses of the skipper I don't mean physical infirmities but flaws in leadership. A gale is no occasion for ignorance of what to do or for timidity in getting it done. Keeping up morale is a categorical imperative: whatever desperate thoughts chase through his mind, the good skipper appears confident, smiles as though enjoying himself, and never lets the genie of panic peep from its bottle. He also tries not to tire himself out, for fatigue erodes judgment.

A sound vessel that has been well taken care of and is commanded by somebody who has prepared himself by wide reading and systematic thinking beforehand is unlikely to come to grief in a gale. Those on board may even be able to find compensation for their discomfort in the wild majesty of the scene, relief from their unease in the noble rise of the bow after every plunge into green water. A flawed vessel in the charge of a person who has not before encountered a gale either in reality or in informed imagination nevertheless stands a good statistical chance of survival—unless the skipper does something extraordinarily stupid—but the crew will have had a terrifying ordeal to no purpose.

Heavy Weather Sailing by K. Adlard Coles is the best introduction to the subject of its title I know of. Its author is an English sailor of enormous experience who has distilled from that experience and the writings of others a number of conclusions and recommendations that make great sense. From this book it is possible to acquire a feeling of what it is like when a gale strikes, and numerous examples document every observation Coles makes. *Heavy Weather Sailing* rings true in terms of my own experience of storms at sea, and reading it has given me added confidence in my ability to take the sea at its worst.

Because so much is made of gales in books on sailing and in conversations with sailors, the novice is likely to form an exaggerated impression of how common they are. In most parts of the world, gales are actually quite rare during their respective sailing seasons and very seldom indeed occur without enough warning for a sailboat either to reach shelter or to get far enough offshore to be able to cope in whatever way seems appropriate. For instance, during an average July less than four hours of winds of Force 8 or more occur between Cape Hatteras and Nova Scotia. The approach of winter brings a turn for the worse: during an average November the same region can expect 50 hours of Force 8 or more, during an average February 115 hours. During April such winds are

back to 50 hours on the average, and during May down to only 15 hours.

I have had my share of foul weather at sea, and each encounter with nature gone mad has had its lesson to teach. Two ordeals I have thus far been spared. One is a sudden onshore gale with neither sea room nor shelter to leeward. The other is a hurricane in deep water accompanied by towering waves with steep breaking crests, unstable mountains down whose fronts rush avalanches of tumbling water whose assault will stagger a lucky boat in their path, overturn an unlucky one.

My first experience of really heavy weather came in an August race in the sloop *Petrouchka*. The course was a counterclockwise circumnavigation of Long Island with the start off Rockaway in the early evening. A hurricane had been moving north during the previous week, but its eye was supposed to pass well east of Cape Cod and head out to sea on the day of the start. When the gun went off the calm ocean, clear sky, and fading breeze combined to portend a tranquil night.

By midnight it was obvious 115

Angry sky usually means angry weather. Boats opposite have already reduced sail. Schooner below is overdue for sail change; heavy swell is sign of still more wind to come.

One man's gale may be another
man's fine sailing breeze.
Unequivocal wind means fast
passage for able boat.
Fair-weather yachtsmen miss half
the fun of sailor's world,
nor can dry land ever seem
half so sweet to them.

that the hurricane had thrown away the Weather Bureau's script and had begun to improvise. A huge swell was now running, the wind was picking up, and a radio bulletin confirmed our guess that the hurricane was swerving westward. To seek shelter on the inhospitable south shore of Long Island was out of the question, and we headed southeast to gain sea room before the real blow began.

The race ceased to be a consideration. We changed the genoa directly to the storm jib, though it was not yet really necessary. We rolled the main down carefully, but even sandwiching in an extensive collection of sailbags and towels could not keep the end of the boom out of the cockpit where it menaced the helmsman's head. When the tail of the hurricane finally struck, we were pretty much ready for it, we thought.

The seas built rapidly and as the boat rose and fell with them the wind slashed at us in spurts that defied all attempts to control the boat or to hold it steady. Every minute or two we were lifted bodily and then flung aside contemptuously by a passing wave. The darkness magnified the scream of the wind and the whine of the rigging. Spray raked the deck and stung bare skin as hail does. So unrelenting was the attack on the senses that I found consecutive thought all but impossible. My mind seemed paralyzed. To formulate the simplest plan was a struggle, to communicate it to the others a feat.

It soon became obvious even in our befuddled state that the sails were doing us no good. We got the storm jib down with no trouble in the trough between two hulking seas and lashed it on the foredeck. The main was more of a problem. The slides were Teflon cylinders that fit inside a groove in the aluminum mast, a clever idea on paper but dreadful in real life. Too little downward pull and nothing happened, too much and the slides would jam. For what seemed a long time—it could have been anywhere from two minutes to fifteen or twenty—Dick and I grappled with the mainsail, our safety belts secured to the mast as we struggled to capture the flailing Dacron with numb fingers. Finally it was down and we bound it to the boom with the tail of the mainsheet.

The wind was offshore and we had seen no ships in several hours, so there seemed no point to staying on deck. Sealed

Rare is sailor who
has never echoed Gonzalo's
plaint in The Tempest:
"Now would I give a
thousand furlongs of sea
for an acre of barren
ground: long heath,
brown furze, anything."

up down below everybody became seasick, but the noise was muffled and it was easier to wedge ourselves against the motion. The ship was taking it all beam-on to the seas, and it was clear that she was far less unhappy left to her own devices than she had been when we tried to force her this way or that.

In the morning the wind fell to manageable proportions, though the waves remained high and confused. Somehow we roused ourselves from the stupor we had fallen into and reset the sails to head back to New York. In The Narrows we joined a procession of other refugees from the race on the way home. As I recall, less than a quarter of the fleet finished the race, and there were numerous sails blown out and at least one dismasting.

Never again will I venture out with a hurricane in the vicinity, regardless of what path may be forecast for it. If I have a roller reefing mainsail, it will have a row of eyelets to permit a good double reef to be taken, and in any case it will have slides that slide and a downhaul as insurance. Lastly I will never hesitate to take down all sail and let the boat take care of herself in moderately bad weather if there is enough sea room and no danger from shipping; though in a really terrible storm where survival is at stake running with the wind is probably safer.

The worst storm I have thus far experienced at sea occurred in November, 1961, on the way from City Island to Norfolk. Perhaps it only felt like the worst, because I had gone to great lengths to assure good weather for that passage and the storm was totally unexpected.

A colleague of mine at New York University was both a sailor and a research meteorologist with access to up-to-the-minute weather information. He kindly undertook to advise me when a good weekend for the run south was in prospect, and I had lined up three friends able at short notice to join my wife and myself to make an adequate complement for *Minots Light*.

October went by with dire prognostications every Thursday but, perversely, fine sailing weather on the actual weekends. Committed as we were to a passage south—*Minots Light* was to spend the winter at Great Bridge, Virginia, for a complete overhaul and face-lift—the unplanned

121

Reefing is basic procedure
practiced by realistic
sailor in advance of need.
Roller reefing is less
trouble than points reefing,
but if reef is deep one,
sail does not always set
so well afterward.

day sails we had on these weekends were in a way something for nothing, a bonus tacked on to an already full season. On one sapphire Sunday a cold brisk wind sent us on a joyous gallop to Port Jefferson and back, a perfect day compounded of fire and ice. I forgave my friend his warnings of tempest that weekend, but by the beginning of November I was growing impatient.

Finally one Thursday brought encouraging news: the coming weekend looked as though it might be just right for our purposes. Friday morning brought confirmation of the forecast of mild, fair winds, and I phoned the others, arranged for a sitter to stay with the children, and knocked off work at noon. By four o'clock *Minots Light* was edging out of her berth at City Island, and soon we were coursing down the East River helped by an ebb tide in full spate. White faces stared at us from every car window: what unworthy fun to picture the crumpled fenders that must have marked our passage, the discontented men who would snarl at their wives that night.

As darkness fell we weaved in and out of the dense harbor traffic, ships and tugs, ferries and pilot boats all intent on their errands. Three of us were professional physicists, trained to discern order in apparent chaos, yet no hint of the Rules of the Road could we find in the behavior of the vessels around us. *Minots Light* under sail might have been a drifting gull for all the attention anybody paid.

The ocean was calm that night, but we were all too excited to get much sleep. Foolishly we sat huddled in the cockpit, talking of everything and nothing in an aura of warm fellowship. A surly dawn accompanied by a rising northwest wind came as a shock; this was not part of The Plan. By noon we were down to forestaysail and main, on course down the Jersey coast and unable to make good our squandered rest in the tumultuous seas that were building up. The radio warned of a severe gale to come. We took in the main and set the mizzen, and later the mizzen came down to leave only the small boomed forestaysail up. With over forty knots of wind behind the beam, we smashed along at eight knots, sometimes nine. It seemed pointless not to make full use of the wind, which at least was in the right direction.

*Foredeck in heavy
weather is no
place for faint-hearted.
Matching rhythm of
task to motion of boat
is key to doing
difficult jobs safely
and rapidly. Proper
oilies are blessing and
ought to be yellow
or orange for visibility.*

Challenge of squall is hard to resist in sound boat with good crew. But the sea is harsh with fools and boldness must give way to prudence if squall is herald of a gale.

Toward evening rain began to fall and we were reminded of how poor visibility had become when a ship first came into sight barely a mile away. To try to make the little harbor of refuge at Cape May seemed a poor idea, and we prudently headed farther offshore despite the worse seas that hunted there. During dinner a loud clap signaled the fracture of the clew fitting on the forestaysail boom. It was blowing Force 9, maybe 10, and the foredeck was sluiced with green water as Alec, Dixon, and I struggled with the flapping forestaysail. What to do next? Under bare poles we were moving at five knots or thereabouts, and Germaine reported no problem at the helm. We continued under bare poles, thankful that no further exertion up forward was necessary.

That night was a horror, compounded by uncertainty as to our position. Dead reckoning is seldom much good in a storm, and the boat was so unsteady that radio direction finder fixes were virtually useless. The situation called for an alert navigator with a disciplined mind adept at inspired guesswork. I felt torpid, my mind was sluggish in the uproar, making it hard to focus on a problem and harder still to force to a conclusion. The simplest calculation took forever to carry out and was subject to gross blunders. The markings on the chart blurred every minute or two, and I stared passively for longer and longer intervals at the rain and spray whose machine-gun attack on the window a foot away was only interrupted by the bomb-bursts of green water from which I flinched instinctively.

The wind continued to increase, and there were moments when the boat seemed about to broach to as we slithered down steep wave faces. I don't recall how fast we were going—the log is incomplete—but I remember clearly that it seemed too fast under the circumstances.

The classic remedy in this situation is to stream lines astern. We used the two jib sheets since they were already on deck, each a hundred-foot length of five-eighths Dacron. What a difference they made! The boat slowed down and the pull of the lines steadied her course markedly. I now believe we could have continued safely with no lines astern, taking the seas on the quarter as they came, had we not been so tired. But streaming the lines made it much less hair-raising to steer, and was clearly the right thing to have done then.

What thoughts does one have during a spell of such heavy weather? Nothing very profound, in my case at least. Probably my reactions were not typical, though, because as owner and master my responsibility was the greatest. Much of the time I ran through in my mind all the catastrophes that might occur, from personal injuries through dismasting, and rehearsed the measures to be taken if they materialized.

I did not dwell on what would happen if someone fell overboard or if the ship were to founder. The first of these was, in any case, too terrible to think about for long, since a person overboard in such a seaway would almost certainly have been lost. But it was also not a likely event, since we invariably used safety belts on deck and were in general safety-conscious. And *Minots*

127

Light is large and heavy, a relatively stable working platform well-fenced with bulwarks, lifelines, and pulpits. Of course we had a routine in mind for trying to recover a man overboard; the point is that it did not dominate my thoughts.

As for foundering, *Minots Light* has a welded-steel hull and a very solid steel-framed superstructure. The deckhouse windows had plywood shutters bolted over them, we had a supply of soft wooden plugs for all through-hull fittings, and so forth. The three bilge pumps—a small electric one, a hand-operated Edson diaphragm pump, and a large Jabsco pump driven through a clutch by the main engine—could cope with a considerable influx of water. Just in case, an inflatable life raft equipped with food, water, and flares was secured on deck with pelican hooks for quick release. So the prospect of sinking remained far back in my mind. But I must have splinted a hundred fractured limbs and fractured booms in my mind while the storm went on.

Besides mulling over possible disasters, I remember wondering more than once just why the hell I was out there. It seemed *wrong* to be so miserable after John Alden had gone to so much trouble to design a lovely yacht, after Abeking and Rasmussen had built her so stoutly, and after I myself had shelled out so much in time and money to perfect her. Why wasn't I at that very moment sailing in warm sunshine toward the indistinct cone of a tropical island just in sight? This endless storm seemed like punishment, but for what crime? Perhaps for believing that meteorology is an exact science. I mourned the prospective loss of a wife and three friends who would surely jump ship when we finally made port, each taking an oar to carry inland resolved not to stop until asked what that strange implement was. Now and then I caught someone looking at me with a calculating expression, and I wondered if I would be sacrificed to the gods of the sea in exchange for relief from the unrelenting wind.

Was I not overwhelmed emotionally by the grandeur of the experience, by the procession of monstrous waves progressing inexorably from nowhere to nowhere? Not quite. It was indeed an awesome spectacle, but after a while it just stopped registering. What never palled was the wild thrill of surfing down a wave front, white rooster tails on either side of the counter. Looking aft from the pulpit I would watch a great sea approach and lift the stern, then the boat would catapult forward with a deep hiss that overrode the howl of the wind. Finally the crest would pass by and the stern would settle back, only to rise again as another sea came up. With a long, straight keel, so unfashionable these days, *Minots Light* gave no real anxiety at the wheel, and even the least proficient of us could control her. It was a pleasure to see a good helmsman at work from my perch forward, carefully aligning the boat to run true with a minimum of correction.

On Sunday morning the wind moderated (if that is the word) to Force 8 and we headed southwest to look for Cape Charles at the southern end of the Delaware peninsula. We recovered the lines—quite a job—and hoisted the forestaysail loose-footed. In the afternoon we found the Chesapeake Light Vessel (now a fixed tower) and turned west into Chesapeake Bay with the help of the engine for a jolting ride toward the entrance to the Intracoastal Waterway.

The bay was completely white, and we saw only one ship under way there during the whole afternoon. We made the lock just after sunset, and it was dark when we finally tied up at the Atlantic Yacht Basin. Never before or since has the simple act of standing on a pier given so much satisfaction.

Monday morning Alec, Dixon, and Ellen left for New York, and Germaine and I began the sad job of stripping the boat for the winter. The only damage had been to the forestaysail boom clew fitting. We had had an ordeal none of us has forgotten, but each of us is still sailing, and *Minots Light* remains in our affectionate regard.

Since that Atlantic gale I have been in a number of other storms offshore, but none so severe. I did not enjoy any of them, but I could face them with a certain degree of equanimity since I knew the ship and I had been through worse. The best thing about having survived thoroughly nasty weather is that thereafter one knows that sooner or later the noise will stop, the sea will flatten, and the sun will come out, with only crusts of salt on deck as reminders of what went before. Every storm has an end.

7/Night

Sailing

At nightfall the world shrinks to a sphere a boat length across whose center is the red glow of the compass. Stars appear, lights flicker along a distant shore, yet the feeling of isolation persists. The air is suddenly chilly, its texture different. The wind is no longer friendly, but instead full of subtle menace. The sea, barely visible, gives no hint of its intentions. Only the ship remains faithful, a steadfast ally whatever lies in store.

The senses become more acute in darkness. Every sound carries a message. The flap of a sail invites its sheet to be trimmed. A creak somewhere forward, a change in the tempo of water rushing past the counter together mean an increase in speed. A hum appears. Was the propeller shaft locked? Yes. What then? It must be the refrigerator, normally inaudible in the cockpit. After a while the hum stops abruptly, and only the hiss of the wake and the slap of waves against the hull can be heard.

Time passes slowly. Six muted chimes signal 2300 and another hour to go.

The compass reads 170°. That's funny, the course is supposed to be 160°. Understanding comes like a splash of cold water, and the wheel is swung over to port. No more dozing. Let's see, there is Sagittarius off the bow, Virgo to starboard, the Big Dipper and Cassiopeia astern. Where is Jupiter? Soon that game palls and another takes its place: the perfect breakfast. Orange juice versus half a grapefruit. Poached eggs versus scrambled. Bacon versus grilled sole. Or maybe a small steak. Toast versus fresh rolls. . . .

Something feels wrong. A glance at the wind sock shows that the wind has freed a little and the sheets must be let out. The wheel is locked and first the jib, then the main, and finally the mizzen are eased. Now the helm is lighter and the speed has picked up. Seven knots. Not bad.

After an eternity a light goes on in the cabin. It is five to twelve. As eight bells strike the next watch comes on deck. It is good to see him, but a trace of resentment is also felt. He is an intruder in what had been a wholly personal universe. Fixed and flashing lights are identified for the newcomer, a minute or two of discussion on how things

*Opening pages: Sunset is
magic interval at sea, last chance
to savor real world
before darkness transmutes
it into distant dream.
In tropics night falls quickly,
in high latitudes transition
is almost imperceptible.*

are going, and finally the wheel is relinquished. Every joint is stiff. Down below the dead-reckoning plot is advanced on the chart, a few notes are entered in the log, a cup of hot bouillon is savored. At last the sack.

My first night passage was made on Long Island Sound, ghosting westward along the Connecticut shore. My two companions were asleep below. They had left New York tired and had had too much to drink on the train. The darkness and the gentle rocking of the boat finished the job. Nothing could have roused them. I did not mind. I had invited them along as insurance against hard weather, and I was happy not to have to share the languorous night with them.

Our pace would have been frustrating in daylight but suited my mood just then. There was barely enough breeze to fill the sails. From time to time a wisp of stouter wind would heel the boat and multiply the bubbles in her wake. A red light appeared off the starboard bow, vanished, reappeared. Was it the running light of another vessel? A buoy? The neon sign of a bar on shore? Reluctantly I reached for the binoculars. It hardly seemed to matter, since we

were afloat on a dream sea in which nothing could happen to disturb our placid progress.

The compass was under a window in the floor of the cockpit, making it a minor effort to examine. This arrangement has its advantages, especially at night when it discourages the helmsman from staring fixedly at the compass to the detriment of his night vision and alertness. I steered at first by whatever star was in line with the jibstay on the right course, periodically shifting to a new one as the night wore on. Past Bridgeport I used a succession of lighthouses as guides, and eventually the distant glow of New York City.

The struggle to stay awake became acute after midnight. At about 0100 I was enveloped in a dense cloak of drowsiness. With what remained of my wits I hardened in the forestaysail until the boat was in perfect balance, then ducked below. The rhythmic sounds of deep sleep told me I could expect no help from the occupants of the cabin. I made a cup of instant coffee and took it and a box of cookies on deck. They helped. Before long the first tentative signs of sunrise appeared behind us. By 0400 it was evident that

133

Dawn is always welcome no
matter how pleasant
the night. Return of sun
brings rebirth of
vigor, rekindling of
spirits, also breakfast.
Morning is time to
check gear and clean ship.

the sun had made a firm decision to appear, and half an hour later it peeped above the horizon.

As we approached Hart Island my slumbering friends returned to life. They craved breakfast. I told them to make it. They seemed to resent the idea, or perhaps the task baffled them. Off City Island the man speared the mooring neatly and helped me get the sails down. When his mate had finished reconstructing her face, we rowed ashore. They drove off at once, while I stayed behind a few minutes longer to watch a new breeze ruffle the surface of Eastchester Bay.

A week later I was crewing on a friend's yawl in an overnight race on the Sound. The boat was unfamiliar, the skipper a perfectionist (as was proper), and I was anxious to avoid mistakes. The night after the start was cold, and the low cockpit coamings offered neither protection nor support. But it was overwhelmingly satisfying to rediscover the lights along the Connecticut shore, here flashing in syncopated cadence, there occulting as though pausing for breath now and then.

A firm northeaster gave a character to the events wholly different from that of the previous passage. We wore oilies and seaboots, and the safety harnesses were as essential in the shallow cockpit as on the foredeck. I had a queasy feeling that hinted at the onset of seasickness. As we beat up the Sound we tacked frequently to stay in the lee of the land where the water was less unruly. When not steering, my job was to tend the running backstays, devilish things that led to winches on each side of the cockpit. It was hard work that had to be done with precision. All this was not my idea of fun and I soon developed a strong wish to be elsewhere, especially when the boat would hit a wave at just the right angle to send a stream of ice water in my face and down my neck.

After four hours the other watch, bulky in heavy sweaters under their oilies, squeezed one by one through the companionway. With no time wasted in idle chatter we retreated below. The others struggled out of their safety harnesses and then fought off their outer garments. I went straight to the sack fully clothed. I could see no advantage in giving up ten minutes of lying down in order to dress and undress in a lurching

135

Winds are sly in darkness,
shifting in direction
and changing in strength as
watch on deck is occupied
with grave philosophical matters.
Night is when friendships
deepen on cruise,
prizes are won or lost in race.

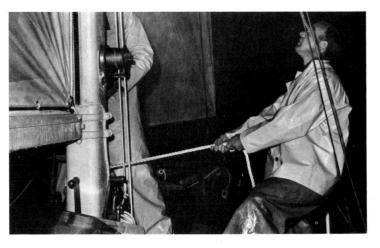

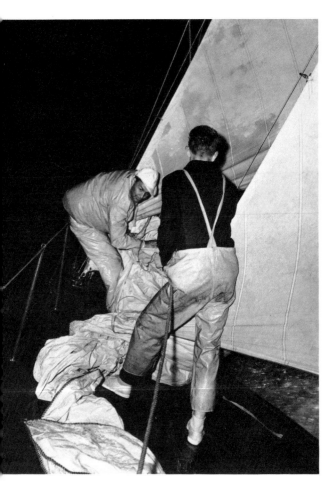

Working the ship continues through the night. Racing, each watch should be able to accomplish by itself such routine chores as changing headsails. Cruising, these tasks usually can be left until next watch appears.

cabin full of hard corners; I still can't. And I like the feeling of being able to go up on deck without delay, ready for anything if need be.

Alas, I had a forward bunk, and rest, let alone sleep, was impossible as the bow slammed into the seas. At least on deck I had been busy at a serious task, not spending all my efforts merely to stay in place. Once or twice I managed to doze off, only to be jarred awake when the boat went about. Round and round in my mind went the phrase, "This way I can play the mast," which had been the skipper's answer to my query as to why he preferred those damned backstay winches to levers. I had not pursued the matter further for fear of displaying my ignorance, and now I wondered just how one plays a mast, and why.

Finally I gave up and, with the help of the safety harness, made a batch of scrambled eggs and toast in time for the next change of watch. This simple task took an absurd amount of time, but it gave me something to do, kept my hands warm, and earned me a disproportionate amount of good will from my shipmates.

On deck once more, a hot breakfast under my belt and a gray dawn breaking, I felt less depressed. The winch handle was an old friend now, and a well-executed tack gave pleasure. We spotted other boats not far away, most of which gave us time; there was no question that plugging away had paid dividends. Soon the wretched discomfort of the night faded from consciousness, and my chief memory was of the intense excitement of driving to windward in the dark against unseen rivals. Sailing was again wonderful: how could I have doubted it only a few hours earlier?

Since then I have spent many nights under sail. Some were in the open Atlantic, each with a grandeur of its own as befits anything to do with an ocean. Unforgettable were runs up the Jersey coast to reach New York Harbor at first light and then to sail up the East River past an eerily silent city. Memories of balmy Mediterranean nights surface every winter, especially of that magic one on which a soft warm breeze wafted us down a placid Tyrrhenian Sea past the spitting fire of Stromboli.

Night watches always seem to be special occasions, rarely lacking in the spice of danger to accentuate the flavor of being under way. Danger is probably too strong a word; uncertainty, or perhaps mystery, is more accurate. Even when I know exactly where I am and where I am headed, and every light in view is accounted for, I still feel a prickle of doubt as I look around, no doubt an echo of some primitive instinct that played a part in the survival of man in the early millennia of his history.

It is well worth while for every sailor to spend a night out in good conditions just to learn what is involved, apart from the pleasure of doing so, on someone else's boat if his own is not suitable. Then he will be prepared in the event of being caught out by a sudden foul wind or reduced visibility. And he may find himself with a new-found yen for a real offshore voyage.

It is always a good idea to set definite watches on a night passage, even on a casual cruise with plenty of people on board. In my experience three hours is about the limit for one man on deck unless there is automatic steering of some kind, in which case four hours may be all right. Two people who are not tired should find alternating every three (or four) hours on a quiet night to be entirely feasible. If they have trouble in staying awake after a while, watches even shorter than three hours are worth a try. By 0200 many people fall into a deep sleep at once when off watch, which enables them to benefit from a short spell in the sack even though earlier they could not have got any real rest in an hour and a half or two hours.

With three watchkeepers on a three-on, six-off schedule there is no problem at all, and those off watch can even be called out once in a while to help on deck without much loss in general efficiency. A crew of four can have a two-on, six-off schedule, or a three-on, six-off schedule with one man out of watch to navigate and act as a reserve. The latter is the procedure we follow on *Minots Light* when two couples are aboard and it seems to work well.

Two people on deck at night when there is nothing to be done except steer, keep a lookout, and occasionally adjust a sheet is a waste, unless it is warm and peaceful enough for one of them to catnap on the lee side of the cockpit. Sleep is a precious commodity. Of course it is more fun to have com-

At night it is especially
important to be sure
of position. Late-afternoon
sight—still better, a
three-star fix at twilight—
means sound sleep for
navigator, is also insurance in
case next day is overcast.

141

Anxiety is companion of helmsman on first coastwise passages in darkness. Each identified aid to navigation is a cherished friend, each steady glow of red or green a hostile stranger. With experience comes confidence, but to relax is dangerous at night when land is near.

pany on deck, and to exchange profound ideas against a backdrop of glittering stars, but every time I have stayed up unnecessarily I have regretted it later.

In many parts of the world it is easier to make a good landfall at night than during the day. Coastal profiles are rarely distinctive, whereas lighthouses and offshore towers can be positively identified. I am happiest in unfamiliar waters when I can approach the shore in darkness, sure of my position, and then enter the harbor or channel that is my goal at daybreak. I dread those situations where I am not quite sure of where I am as I close with an ambiguous coast in the late afternoon and then have to find my way past unlit hazards (fish traps, sunken wrecks, broken pilings, abandoned piers) in darkness in search of a berth.

One close shave occurred in the Ionian Sea. The archipelago off the Dalmatian coast had turned out to have been more to our liking than anywhere else in the Mediterranean, and all of us were reluctant to

142

leave that paradise of fragrant green islands surrounded by crystalline waters and sparsely populated by friendly people who nevertheless respected our privacy. We had already explored the Italian coast on the way to Yugoslavia. The plan was therefore to leave Gruz, the harbor of Dubrovnik, at the last possible moment, and to get back to our base at Palma de Mallorca either nonstop or with a single stop at Cagliari in Sardinia to refuel if we were compelled to motor a lot.

We left Gruz under power with a northeast wind just strong enough to blow the exhaust into the cockpit. The autopilot was in a cooperative mood, and all hands sprawled over the foredeck to restore their tans in those places where they had faded while we were in Gruz. At lunchtime the wind began to back to the northwest and to harden, and in the afternoon we were able to stop the engine and reach down the Adriatic under all plain sail plus mizzen staysail.

Good visibility and open water meant no problems that night, and by morning we were off Otranto, at the heel of the Italian boot. The wind vanished entirely soon afterward, and we spent the rest of the morning and most of the afternoon under standard Mediterranean rig of awnings, autopilot, and engine. The day was hot, and I rigged a hose from the deckwash pump to a spray head clamped to the now-idle jibstay to provide saltwater showers. It was stifling below, and we stayed on deck to read, talk, play chess, and to finish the fruit that had been expected to last until Palma. The wake extended in a straight line behind us exactly as the advertisements show.

At 1720 a wind came up from the south, and we got the awnings down and the sails up. The barograph trace had begun to drop and cirrus clouds were accumulating in the sky. An hour later a full-fledged sirocco rattled the shrouds and we roared along under main, jib, and forestaysail on the port tack toward Capo Rizzuto. The sea soon became lumpy and at sunset I decided to head for Crotone, now thirty miles away. This was supposed to be a pleasure trip, after all, and anyway it would be interesting to visit the city where Pythagoras and his followers had done their most important work.

Finding Crotone was easy, and just before midnight we took the sails down and headed in with the light at the end of the breakwater just off the port bow. Suddenly all the lights in the city went out. I felt a sudden stab of fear and spun the wheel hard over to starboard. A moment later the city lights went on again, and now I could see where the high breakwater had been extended a few hundred feet beyond the light. We had just missed smashing into it in the darkness.

Crotone is not the only place where aids to navigation may prove to be the contrary. Buoys everywhere are sometimes missing or out of position, beacons that mark rock outcrops may be too camouflaged by gull droppings to be discernable from a distance. Light vessels, now fortunately on their way out, are notorious offenders.

Some years ago my wife and I and two friends left Miami to sail north. Our plan was to stay offshore as long as possible to make use of the considerable Gulf Stream current, and we hoped to continue as far as Morehead City before entering the Intracoastal Waterway. Late on the second day out the wind, initially from the southeast, shifted to the north and an unpleasant sea built up rapidly. We decided to make for the nearest safe entrance to the Waterway.

Dead reckoning is not very accurate in the Gulf Stream, since the speed of the latter varies from place to place and from time to time, but I had been keeping track of our position by occasional sun-sights and radio-beacon bearings. The Georgia and Carolina coasts are flat and featureless with outlying shoals, so we decided to head for the Savannah Light Vessel first. I thought we could simply home in on its radio beacon, and the timing was such that we ought to pick up its light about midnight. A sound plan for a difficult coast, but I could not get the radio beacon on the RDF when we should have been within range. Still, I had obtained a reasonably good celestial fix at twilight, so we kept on toward where the chart said the light vessel lay.

By midnight there was no light visible anywhere, fixed or flashing, no radio-beacon signal, and the depth sounder indicated only sixty feet of water. What to do? We were all tired because of the boat's motion and not a little alarmed to find ourselves lost. Dave made a brilliant suggestion: why not anchor until daybreak? It seemed strange to anchor in the open ocean out of sight of land, but it ought to be safe enough if not very comfortable. We took in the sails and anchored with plenty of line out, had a hasty supper, and despite the bobbling around fell asleep immediately. We did not keep an anchor watch—we had seen no shipping for some time, the masthead light was on, the wind had died down to Force 3, and the anchor had dug itself in well—but every hour one or another of us became sufficiently uneasy to wake up and go on deck for a look around anyway. The next day, refreshed, we sailed west until we could see land and then went parallel to the coast while watching the depth sounder until we found the buoys marking an inlet near Savannah.

The day after that we finally discovered the Savannah Light Vessel securely tied to a pier in Charleston. She had been withdrawn from service for an overhaul two days before, but the relief vessel had not gone out at the same time because of the same norther that had sent us in search of her.

8 Nav

igation

Navigating a sailboat is a game in which success often requires luck as well as skill. To win the game is to make a perfect landfall after a passage in open water; to lose is to run down the predicted distance and find a wall of rock in place of a harbor, a blank horizon in place of a welcoming island. Along the way are minor contests with prizes of their own to keep the navigator's spirits up, such as a three-star fix that yields a cocked hat a pencil point across.

The progress of a sailboat through the water is never entirely predictable. The course derived from the chart may be perfectly correct, but it is hard to estimate leeway accurately, to allow the right amount for tidal set, and to gauge steering error. Something is always lost when tacking, but how much and in what direction? Few compass deviation cards can be trusted to better than a degree or two. A mile here, a mile there. Fortunately it is rare for all the departures from an estimated course made good to occur in the same direction, but such a coincidence is possible and must be allowed for in plotting a course under sail.

The problems of the sailboat navigator are too anachronistic to be considered in most textbooks, let alone to form the core of the exposition. I feel that the overriding consideration is to build into every course, either proposed for the future or conjectured for the past, a healthy allowance for uncertainty. The worst moment for the navigator —well, one of the worst, there are plenty of other candidates—is to complete the plotted journey and know neither where he is nor in which direction his destination lies. The wise navigator draws on the chart not only the direct course from his point of departure to his destination, including a correction for any currents along the way, but also lines on either side that represent his guess as to the limits of the actual course that might result.

Often I don't even try to make a perfect landfall but instead deliberately head over to one side well beyond the limit of any misjudgment of leeway or poor estimates by helmsmen of courses made good. Then, when land is sighted, I know just which way to turn even though the exact dis-

Opening pages: Navigator is priest of sailor's religion, first conducting mysterious rites with sacred objects and then prescribing correct path for salvation. In time of stress, navigator is first to be consulted, is always ready to claim credit for successful voyage. He may even deserve some, too.

tance left may be uncertain. If this fail-safe scheme can be combined with staying to windward of the destination, it is hard to see what is to be gained by sailing a direct course in any but the best circumstances.

Estimating leeway is not a trivial problem. Even the most cunning design of the underwater body of a hull cannot produce an infinite resistance to lateral motion, and some leeway is inevitable when sailing to windward. The navigator who simply ignores leeway should not be surprised to find himself a mile off course for every ten or twelve miles spent on the wind, even more when it blows up.

How much leeway can be expected? A really close-winded boat such as a 12-meter can make good a course about 3° to leeward of the course steered; a modern cruising boat with good all-round performance might exhibit a leeway angle of about 5° when all goes well. Heeling and pinching increase leeway markedly. And in severe conditions, just when accurate navigation is most essential, the usual leeway made by a boat is magnified to an unpredictable extent by the increase in side force due to distortion of the sails, by the need to bear off frequently to maintain speed in a seaway when the sails are blanketed in the troughs, and by the effect of wind-driven surface drift of the sea itself. Leeway may total 10° or even 15° as a result.

Wind-driven surface drifts occur only in the upper few feet of the ocean and hence do not affect ships. Accordingly almost no attention has been paid to them, but the sailboat navigator has good reason to keep them in mind offshore. These drifts are fickle affairs that shift in direction and speed with the local wind and are not to be confused with such large-scale ocean currents as the Gulf Stream.

Surface drifts seem to amount to two or three percent of the wind speed. This may not appear like much, but a drift of half a knot, corresponding to a wind of twenty knots or so, is hardly negligible. The drift is not in the same direction as that of the wind because of the effect of the earth's rotation, but is displaced by 20° to 40° to the right of the wind in the northern hemisphere, the same amount to the left of the wind in the southern. Hence in the northern hemisphere

149

Top: With two wheels and assortment of dials, helmsman of this boat has plenty to keep him busy; fixed chart table is worth having. Above: View from cockpit of 12-meter Heritage; *radar reflector is good idea in poor visibility. Right: Instruments on* Minots Light *are conveniently placed.*

one goes slower but points higher on the port tack and goes faster but makes more leeway on the starboard tack; the reverse holds for the southern hemisphere. More than one dead-reckoning position has been grossly in error because surface drift was disregarded.

Sailboat instrumentation ranges from a pair of yarn telltales on a dinghy to an electronic array as extensive as that of any ship on a large cruising ketch. The irreducible minimum for any self-respecting boat is a compass. If passages are contemplated, even fairly short runs, a distance log is an essential. It need not be elaborate; the kind in which the turns of a spinner towed behind the boat register on a clock-like dial is quite accurate. A compass and a distance log are all that is needed for dead-reckoning navigation, and it is possible to enjoy a lifetime of coastal passages with no more than these.

With so many variable factors to juggle, the prospect of navigating a sailboat with only a compass and a distance log might seem discouraging. On the contrary, the fact that dead reckoning consists largely of adding an estimate to a guess and then subtracting a surmise only contributes to the fascination of the job. The good navigator brings the flair of a pastry cook as well as dividers and protractor to the chart table. Faced with a polygon of uncertainty the size of Rhode Island, either his intuition will be able to shrink it to manageable proportions or his wit will be able to devise a strategy that sidesteps the problems.

The navigator always has his most anxious moments when nearing land. Here a set of alert senses can cancel out any lack of elaborate instrumentation. Standing clouds in the trade winds speak of islands beneath, at night the murmur of distant surf and the chatter of sea birds hint of land ahead. My wife smelled Ireland before we saw it, and an aroma mingling rosemary, thyme, and myrtle announced the proximity of Corsica despite an early-morning mist that obscured its rugged coastline.

Nevertheless, an upward step in sophistication does add to safety and convenience. A speed log, a depth sounder, and a radio direction finder are all worth having, as is a barograph. The best thing about possessing such devices is the mute reproach they offer the unambitious sailor.

All sailboats make leeway
going to windward. Additional
factor often neglected
is wind-driven drift of sea
surface. Both must be
taken into account in stiff
breeze to avoid being set far to
leeward of desired course.

With them on board, there can be no excuse to remain in home waters, no way to suppress the pull of the horizon.

A speed log is a major aid in getting the best from a sailboat, indeed in learning how to sail properly in the first place, and is a help to the navigator in several ways. The very best speed logs, for instance the Brookes and Gatehouse "Hermes" (called the "Harrier" when combined with a distance log) and the latest Kenyons, are sensitive and accurate and perform to match their cost. But simple logs that consist of a projecting finger mechanically coupled to a cockpit dial are much cheaper and do their job competently.

Depth sounders function by sending out pulses of sound waves and timing the return of echoes from the sea floor. The meter type of depth sounder, for instance the Brookes and Gatehouse "Hecta," is easiest to read in the cockpit, but not wholly reliable, since it shows maximum depth with certain bottoms, when the engine is in reverse, and when not working properly. The type of depth sounder that uses a neon lamp revolving in a circle gives a better indication of the type of bottom—a sharp line when the bottom is hard, a band of light when it is mud or covered with weed—and a malfunction is more obvious, but such an instrument is hard to read in sunlight. I have one of each: a Hecta with a cockpit indicator and a Raytheon neon-lamp sounder in a corner of the deckhouse, and I find both useful. If I had to choose just one, I would take the meter-reading Hecta, because it allows the helmsman to keep an eye on the depth without effort.

A radio direction finder permits lines of position to be derived by rotating its antenna until a null signal is obtained from a known transmitter. Most of the world's coastlines are studded with direction-finding stations, and an RDF is therefore good insurance against getting hopelessly lost within a few dozen miles of the shore. Since RDF bearings are never wholly precise, an RDF fix must always be regarded with skepticism. But it is vastly better than nothing.

The above instruments make a very adequate set for the coastwise cruiser with the addition of a barograph to keep tabs on the weather. A barograph makes a perma-

Fog provides good excuse
for day in harbor.
But passage in fog through
waters free of
shipping is special treat,
not dangerous if
made slowly under sail with
eyes and ears alert.

155

Tidal streams may reach
several knots. In light airs
boats under sail cannot
always stem tide, may have to
anchor to keep from being
swept back. Weaker flow, reverse
eddies are possible near
shore, can help nerveless sailor.

nent record of atmospheric pressure, and permits the sailor to make his own prognoses of weather trends in his vicinity. Unless one is willing to write down its readings every hour round the clock, including a few days before one sets out on a trip, a barometer is virtually useless; put the money aside as a first installment toward a barograph.

Few parts of the world offer such severe tests of a navigator's ability as Maine does on occasion. The coast of Maine is a compound of pink granite and green forest, of remote islands and ravishing coves, all washed by the cold emerald Atlantic which at times asserts its sovereignty with a roar of breaking water and a shower of glinting spray. A magnificent coast, incomparable at its best; a severe coast, not to be taken lightly by any who approach it.

So much has been written about sailing in Maine that a cruise there has something of the flavor of a pilgrimage. If the weather is kind, the reality surpasses all expectation. A cruise in Maine is one of the classic treats of the sailor, in the same category as a trade-wind passage or a tour of the sun-drenched islands of the Mediterranean.

But fog can make Maine a navigator's nightmare. When it is clear, the narrow channels between concealed rock ledges are easy to negotiate by day or by night, and the direction and speed of a tidal stream can be estimated from the wakes left by buoys in its path. When visibility falls to a matter of yards, however, sailing on this coast assumes the status of an adventure.

I first cruised to Maine in the cutter *Nipinke*. We left Mamaroneck at the end of May and proceeded in leisurely fashion Down East. Falmouth Foreside in Casco Bay was our first taste of Maine. Was it my imagination that gave a special tang to the salt air, a special hue to the evergreen woods? We celebrated with a lobster dinner ashore, and that evening a damp gray fog confirmed our arrival in these fabled waters.

Maine has no monopoly of fog, but a genuine Maine pea-souper is something unique, a *thing* and not merely a suspension of water droplets in the air. Nothing around us was visible, not even the boats at nearby moorings. The furled jib alternately faded from sight and reappeared, a ghostly presence in the swirling mist. Soon night fell,

156

and from the cockpit I watched hemispheres of light bulge from the cabin windows. Later, zipped snugly in down-filled sleeping bags, we listened to the steady drip of water that had condensed on the spars and rigging.

In the morning the fog was gone and under a pellucid sky *Nipinke* skipped across Casco Bay. We ran wing-and-wing with mainsail to port and jib to starboard, the tiller feather-light, the helmsman's eyes fixed on the telltales to keep her dead before the southwesterly wind. Visibility was superb, with even distant buoys standing out sharply from the white-flecked water around them.

Two more days like this and *Nipinke* was in Camden, just inside Penobscot Bay. More accurately, she was at anchor in the outer harbor, a long row in a 6-foot pram from the town. But no matter, it is always fun to inspect a fleet of fine yachts at close range and to exchange jovial greetings with their crews as one goes slowly by, simple pleasures denied those who prefer to race past with outboards sputtering.

From Camden to Schoodic

Point at the far end of Frenchman Bay we sailed past hundreds of islands, inlets, and passages, all incomplete without the presence of a sailboat. Some are perpetually crowded and noisy, others are unfrequented for no discernible reason. My own taste is for the latter, but there are exceptions. Northeast Harbor on Mount Desert Island, for instance, somehow manages to gain rather than lose from the swarm of boats that fills it, lured by moorings and a marina, hot showers and a laundromat at the town dock, excellent shopping and Flick Flye's lobsters.

But I like Somes Sound much better. The marshmallow name does it no justice, for it is a dramatic fjord that nearly splits Mount Desert Island in two. (The Norwegians are better at naming fjords, perhaps because they have had more practice.) On one side all is green and rounded, on the other steep rock cliffs drop to the water's edge. A huge notch in these cliffs called Valley Cove makes a spectacular anchorage, though I prefer to go all the way to the head of the sound where the holding is more secure and the view stunning.

That splendid book *A Cruising Guide to the New England Coast*—as welcome a companion on winter evenings as on summer days—considers Eggemoggin Reach less interesting than Deer Isle Thoroughfare or Merchants Row for a passage between Penobscot and Blue Hill bays. It depends on what interests you. Eggemoggin Reach is my favorite, and I will not argue with anyone uncharitable enough to point out that this is because it offers a chance to sail in agreeable surroundings with no problems of navigation or rough seas to contend with.

In *Nipinke* we left Bucks Harbor at the western end of the Reach one morning with the idea of continuing on to Swans Island. When we saw a deserted cove near Brooklin on the mainland shore we could not resist anchoring there. My wife read in the afternoon sun, I watched passing boats and sent out powerful and effective extrasensory messages that kept them from joining us, and the children fed ducks with, as it turned out, our whole supply of bread.

A dense fog enveloped us the following morning, and we rowed ashore for a walk to the town. The fog persisted the entire day, and was still there the morning after

that. Claustrophobia makes risky ventures seem more sensible than they are. There was just enough wind to sail, and buoys with distinctive sound signals marked the way to Northeast Harbor. I made meticulous plots of the tidal streams for the rest of the day, and we set off in the murk.

The allowances for tidal set and leeway were all good enough for us to pick up the assorted clangs and moans of the buoys on schedule, which is really nothing to boast of since the buoys were not all that far apart. Nevertheless, to sail blind for a whole day in the knowledge that an error of judg-

ment will be punished by the crunch of iron on rock is surely the most exciting experience possible while averaging three knots.

Each minute seemed an hour. The hardest job was to keep the children quiet as we strained to locate the faint hee-haw of a distant diaphone. We stiffened with helpless unease as the rumble of an invisible lobster boat approached, passed us, and then receded. Everything on board was wet to the touch and I constantly had to wipe the mist from my glasses. Were those breakers ahead or merely waves slapping against a buoy? Different sounds carry differently through

fog and the sequence of buoys sometimes seemed reversed to our nervous ears. Gradually anxiety was replaced by exhilaration. We began to enjoy ourselves.

As we entered Northeast Harbor we heard disembodied voices, a ship's clock chiming the half-hour, the rattle of oars, a halyard flapping. We made our way among the shadowy masses of moored boats until we spotted a vacant buoy. A shove of the tiller, a flutter of the sails, and it was alongside. In a moment the slimy eye splice was on the samson post and our voyage was over. Hot soup and crackers crisped in the folding oven were our reward.

After another week in the neighborhood of Mount Desert Island we sailed up Somes Sound in a light drizzle to the boatyard at its head and left *Nipinke* in Farnham Butler's capable hands. No yard I know of has so romantic a setting, and I cannot see how anybody there ever gets any work done. But they seem to, for the next spring when we drove up we found *Nipinke* all ready to go, with her freshly-painted topsides reflecting the dancing waves around her. A pearly fog the next day meant challenge, not calamity, and we left to sail down to Manset with no hesitation.

Since then I have made many passages in fog, in Maine and elsewhere, thus far without mishap. Some were deliberate, motivated chiefly by impatience, others simply the result of ill chance en route. To set out from a secure harbor in a fog may be a bold act, but if backed up by the calculations of a prudent navigator and the eyes and ears of an alert crew it need not be a foolish one.

Today a radar scanner sprouts from *Minots Light's* mizzenmast, and hitting a buoy on the nose (figuratively speaking, of course) in a fog is now routine. The radar plus its installation plus the repairs that were needed a month after the warranty expired totaled about as much as *Nipinke* had cost. Though it is still a strain to proceed in poor visibility where shipping abounds, I feel less helpless than before when the hollow blast of a foghorn floods the air. But once in a while I miss the thrill of sailing blind, even the accompanying whiff of danger.

Offshore passages call for a knowledge of celestial navigation, which all landlubbers and many sailors regard as an amalgam of witchcraft and higher mathematics. Visitors to *Minots Light* are always awed by the chronometer gimbaled below a window in the chart table and the two sextants chocked in their own drawer nearby. These instruments are not particularly expensive, and would be instantly recognized by a seaman of the last century. There is nothing spectacular about using them, nor about the calculations that transform the numbers they provide into lines of position on a chart. Yet nobody to whom I attempt to explain the wonders of my truly unique switchboard ever seems to take his eyes off the chronometer, and so dramatic is the response of women to my demonstration of how to use a sextant that my wife prefers their drawer to be locked in her absence.

Celestial navigation is really rather easy despite the meticulousness required, and a full understanding of its principles is not necessary to do a good job. I find it more of a problem to estimate the combined effects of leeway and tidal set accurately, and a fix a few miles in error in the middle of the ocean is hardly likely to have consequences as severe as a similar discrepancy that occurs during a coastwise passage.

But it is impossible to deny the romance of navigating by the sun, moon, stars, and planets. To lean against the mast while bringing the sun down to the horizon in the telescope of a sextant is a delicious act, far more satisfying than turning the loop of a radio direction finder or twirling the knobs of a loran receiver. "Mark!" you cry, and a shipmate writes down the time and the altitude. A few more observations as a check, some hocus-pocus at the chart table, and lo! a line of position as good as gold. The high point of the navigator's day at sea comes when the morning line of position is advanced to cut the latitude revealed by the noon sight. For a moment he is as important as the cook as all hands assemble around the chart table to see where the ship is and how far it has gone since noon of the day before.

Every summer I take sights regularly and work them out even when there is no real need to do so. Though I say I do this to keep in practice, the real reason is that I too enjoy the heft of the sextant, the conjuring trick of drawing that definitive line on the chart.

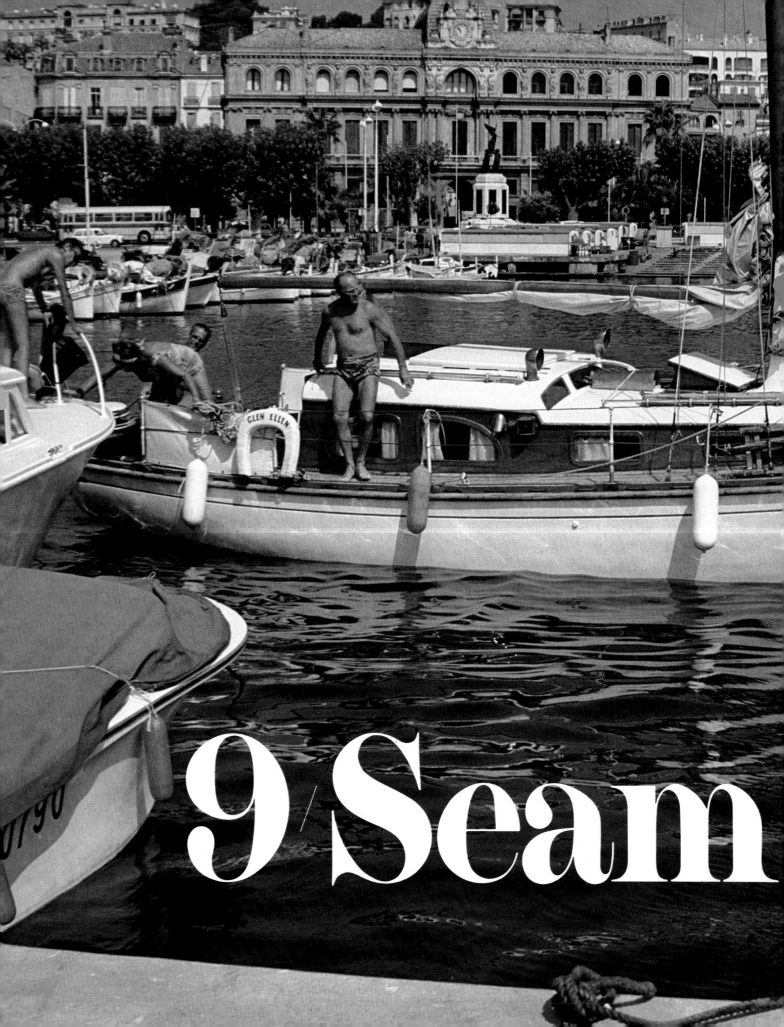

9/Seam

anship

To manage a sailboat properly one must be competent not only in the art of sailing but also in the craft of seamanship and in the science of navigation. To be sure, there is plenty of art, craft, and science in each of these rather arbitrary categories, but I like to distinguish among them by their respective dominant characters. All three are involved to some extent in any sailing venture, from a day sail to an ocean passage, yet my impression is that few yachtsmen value their skills in seamanship to the same extent as their skills in sailing and navigation. This is a pity, because the exercise of seamanship is rewarding when mastered, embarrassing when not.

An important aspect of seamanship concerns handling a boat when its sails are down. The seaman takes over from the sailor when a boat is to be anchored or tied up to a dock, when it goes aground, and so forth—the unglamorous parts of the game.

Anchoring preserves, even enhances, the mood of a cruise; tying up in a marina destroys it. To me, the right way to end a day's sail is to anchor in the late afternoon. It is a delicious moment when the anchor bites into the bottom and the concentration needed while under way slips off like a shed skin. Then comes a swim if it is warm enough, perhaps even if it isn't. A drink may be in order. While dinner is being prepared the sails are shaken out and furled neatly. The sheets are coiled and hung up, and the halyard falls are carried out to the rails to keep them from slapping against the mast. The anchor light is secured to the jibstay. A whipping may have to be replaced, a jib hank reseized, the corner of a batten pocket restitched. If we have been under power for long, I check the fuel and possibly pump some from a reserve tank into one of the main tanks. Final notes on the day's adventures are entered in the log.

By this time dinner is ready, and all hands attack it with relish. Later a cigar on deck in the violet dusk, brandy, music, talk. Plans for the following day are reviewed. A laughing moon sheds silver flakes on the water. I may remember to turn on the anchor light. We go to bed reluctantly and fall asleep at once.

In the morning, first a look around to gauge the weather. I may remember to turn off the anchor light. A plunge over the side shakes loose the remnants of sleep. The cockpit table is set in place to the whine of the coffee grinder in the galley. We breakfast amid bird song and the fragrance of coffee brewing. Mendicant swans glide over to rap their beaks imperiously on the hull for an offering of bread.

Nobody feels ambitious, but habit impels us through the motions of getting ready to leave. The main is cranked up. The windlass makes short work of heaving in the anchor rode. We sail slowly out as the anchor is brought on deck and secured in its chocks. A quick luff and the white triangle of the genoa rises up its stay. Back on course I signal the trim of the sails from the pulpit. Winches click. The boat comes alive as it picks up speed. We round a bend in the channel and the anchorage disappears.

It is not always so idyllic. For every perfect anchorage, there is another with poor holding and worse shelter; for every oasis of peace and privacy, there is another the victim of water-skiers and generators barking without cease. Still, on balance I have spent far more good nights at anchor than bad ones, and to me anchoring is an essential component of the experience of cruising under sail.

Different anchorages require different anchors and different techniques. The one-design racer and the man who spends every night in a marina berth often find it hard to believe that there is more to anchoring than merely dropping a clumsy steel object over the bow. Nevertheless far more yachts have been lost through dragging their anchors than have been lost at sea, and the ignominy of the former fate fully matches the tragedy of the latter. Seamanship consists largely of avoiding avoidable risks, and few cases of dragging are inevitable.

I carry three anchors ready for use at short notice, a large and a small Danforth and a fisherman, and three rodes, one of chain and two of nylon. The large Danforth is the usual choice for overnight or longer, the small one for short periods or to take out in the dinghy when we go aground. The hundred-pound fisherman is in the way on deck and hard to handle in action, but it

165

Sailing into harbor
takes well-coordinated crew and
helmsman familiar
with way the boat behaves.
Here Mustang, *with mainsail reefed*
because of strong wind,
has just dropped jib before
entering anchorage.

sometimes holds in rocky or weed-covered bottoms when the Danforths are no good.

The first time I used the fisherman was on a return passage from Maine to New York. It was already early September, and we had to be back home as soon as possible. We had left Boothbay Harbor with a northeasterly behind us, intending to make directly for the Cape Cod Canal which we figured to reach the next day. At first we had fine sailing across a hilly jade sea, but toward evening the wind increased and heavy rain started to fall. Visibility became poor. The flavor of what had begun as a fine adventure was rapidly turning sour. We just made Gosport Harbor in the Isles of Shoals at dark. Three tries with the Danforth showed it to be useless on the rocky bottom, so I assembled the fisherman, shackled it to the chain, and got it overboard as Germaine struggled to hold *Minots Light* in position. It took hold at once. The anchor watch we kept was a welcome alternative to what would have been a grim night out.

In waters where there is little or no tidal rise and fall, it may be a good idea to take a line ashore when at anchor.

In a crowded anchorage this may permit a yacht to squeeze in when otherwise there would be no room. And many harbors have attractive nooks where one can only lie without swinging. If the shore is bold, it is fun to go in close enough to step ashore directly: *Minots Light* has spent many nights with her bow tied to a tree and an anchor out astern despite her draft of nearly eight feet.

The competent handling of a sailboat in close quarters deserves respect, because it is by no means either easy or common. In his home waters, the skipper of a sailboat will know all the tricks to picking up his mooring or coming into his marina berth, and going alongside the club float or a fuel dock will be an old story to him. In a strange harbor, especially when entered at night or in a strong wind, the problems to be faced are no longer familiar, and it is well for him to understand the basic principles of controlling his unwieldy charge under power.

The great spectator sport at the Club Náutico de Palma de Mallorca is to sit on the terrace late in the afternoon, drink in hand, to watch arriving boats tie up stern-first at the quay a few yards away.

166

Standards are high, but judgment is fair: no blunder goes unnoticed, no virtuoso stroke unappreciated. One July afternoon I sat there with some friends in the shade of the awning to enjoy the forthcoming performances. My interest was not wholly casual, since there was an empty space to port of *Minots Light* and somebody would be sure to try to fill it.

Under the best of conditions, namely flat calm and no current, it is not a simple task to back a sailboat into a narrow berth. Even with a neutral helm, no single-screw vessel will move directly astern when it is in reverse. A propeller gets a better bite on the water in the lower half of each turn. Nearly all auxiliary sailboats have right-hand propellers, that is, propellers that turn clockwise in forward gear when viewed from aft. In reverse the propeller turns counterclockwise, so that the stern of the boat is forced to port. The result is a curved path, never a straight one.

The correct technique for a Mediterranean harbor is therefore to drop the anchor well off the quay with the bow headed to port relative to a direct line to the clear space at the quay. Then, as the boat backs up and the anchor rode is paid out, the stern will gradually swing around until, if all goes well, the boat is perpendicular to the quay when it gets there.

The skipper of the Belgian yawl which was the first to arrive at the Club Naútico must have been aware of all this, but he failed to take sufficient account of the cross wind that was present that day. His boat, like most sailboats, had more windage forward than aft, and the wind from the port side accentuated the tendency of the boat to rotate clockwise. As a result the boat swung around too far despite the skipper's efforts at the wheel, and ended up diagonally across the opening with the stern to windward. Naturally, he shifted to forward gear to get out, but the wind, though not particularly strong, prevented him from making a good escape and the yawl ran crosswise onto *Minots Light's* anchor chain and stuck there.

At this point everybody within sight stopped what they were doing to see what would happen next. Even Gustavo and Juan, the club waiters, lost their usual nonchalance. I felt as much sympathy for the unfortunate skipper as I felt anxiety for *Minots Light*. But he kept his wits and did the only sensible thing, which was to crank in his own anchor chain to pull himself off.

Enlightened self-interest sent me out to *Minots Light's* bow when the Belgian yawl made its second, and much better, attempt. I took a stern line from them and made it fast to a ring on the quay, which enabled them to straighten out the boat and work it into the narrow space available by pushing, pulling, and shouting. The racket was unnecessary; I think the calm skipper deserved a less hysterical crew. Finally, all was secure and I returned to my seat for another gin and tonic.

The next boat to appear was Irving Johnson's *Yankee*. He sailed into Palma's outer harbor under striped genoa, main, mule, and mizzen, a pretty sight, and got the sails in just outside the club's breakwater. As a boy I had pored over Johnson's books and articles, and a lecture of his had been a motivating factor in my bringing *Minots Light* to Europe. So I was curious to see how a master seaman would cope.

Yankee came around the end of the breakwater slowly as her skipper sized up the situation. An opening a few boats over from *Minots Light* was his choice. He went past it, swung around, and the anchor was let go in the right spot with the boat ideally oriented. Then he backed up boldly to prevent the wind from taking charge, gave a short burst in forward to straighten her out at the end, and slid neatly into place—an elegant performance.

Every harbor presents its special problems, even outside the Mediterranean. It is well worth perfecting a routine for docking when there is nobody on shore to help—or, worse, somebody all too eager to help but incompetent to do so. Many, many sad experiences have soured me on dockside volunteers. Usually, Helpful Harry grabs the line thrown to him and, instead of placing the eye at its end over the bollard or cleat indicated to him, insists on pulling the bow in hard. Then, when things are beyond tinkering with and I want to go out and try again, he makes the line fast. Or he takes the line, winds it once around a bollard, and stands back to enjoy the applause as it slowly but surely comes off. Or he just stands there

169

*Above: Self-sufficiency is mark
of good seamanship. With each member
of crew given specific task,
Mariah can enter berth without fuss
after fine day's sail. Below:
Heeling grounded boat further with
help of masthead line reduces
draft and is often best way to get off.*

holding the line in a limp hand, frozen with terror, as if it were a hungry anaconda. Sometimes he won't even pick up the line, although he motioned for it to be thrown to him in the first place. And if, indeed, Harry can be persuaded to just put the eye over a bollard, it is never the one I ask for.

Nowadays I try hard to avoid dockside assistance. If it is impossible to manage without a hand ashore, I somehow get one of my crew there first, perhaps by going alongside another boat for a moment or by coming in bow first and then backing away. In return for the extra effort there is less likelihood of trouble and a pleasant feeling of self-sufficiency.

Getting out of a mess is a more difficult aspect of seamanship than staying clear of one in the first place. Going aground is a good example. It is no joke, however comic it appears to onlookers. Carelessness is the usual cause, but even the most meticulous seaman can be led astray by erroneous local advice, by incorrect charts or buoyage, or by the need to avoid a collision.

I have gone aground countless times, of which I am neither proud nor ashamed. In saying that the most frequent reason was faulty information, I am not trying to shift the blame but to emphasize that skepticism is a healthy habit at sea. Local knowledge has been the worst offender. I still remember getting stuck off Frazers Hog Cay in the Bahamas in a boat drawing five feet while local knowledge on the pier bellowed that the channel was seven feet deep. I remember jolting to a stop in the entrance to Daytona Beach Boat Works in Florida while holding in my hand a letter from the manager stating that ten feet was always available. We drew less than eight feet, and in getting off the rudder was damaged. I remember local knowledge in the harbor of Hanko, Finland, positively guaranteeing three meters least depth; we went aground drawing sixty centimeters less than that. I can go on like this for quite a while. As far as I am concerned, local knowledge is local ignorance.

Charts are not infallible either, sad to say, though their record beats that of local knowledge. In places where silting is to be expected, I am always cautious whatever the chart says: I go slow, stay on the windward side of the channel, and try to time the passage to coincide with a rising tide.

Pinching to windward has taken me aground more often than I like to recall. It is remarkable how much leeway is made while pinching. Usually we bump just as I demand thanks from the others for having saved them the labor of another pair of tacks by my skill at windward sailing. Still vivid in my memory is a warm July evening in Maine when we were beating up Somes Sound against a falling tide in a failing wind just at sunset. So overwhelming was the crystalline perfection of the scene that nobody noticed how much leeway we were making. We were hung up for nearly six hours.

There is no lack of stratagems for getting off, once aground. I have tried them all at one time or another, but there is only one method that stands a real chance of working if full reverse on the engine has no effect and the tide is not rising: take an anchor out toward deep water, set up a healthy strain on it, and then reduce the boat's draft by heeling it over. Swinging the main boom all the way out with someone at its end may be enough, but a more heroic measure has never yet failed me. This in-volves taking a line from the masthead to an anchor well out, to a tree ashore if one is in the right place, or to another boat which by this time has no doubt come to watch.

I am always impressed by the way in which heeling a sailboat by a masthead line can save an otherwise bleak situation. In 1970 *Minots Light* was tearing through the Stockholm archipelago under reaching jib, main, mizzen, and mizzen staysail, over 2500 square feet of sail all pulling mightily on a broad reach. We were doing nine knots with spurts of nearly ten in a strengthening southwesterly. One day like that is enough to make a whole summer worthwhile. Then round a bend, and where there should have been a buoy—nothing. The chart showed the buoy as marking one side of a narrow channel between rock outcrops, with the channel passing close to it. There simply was no time to do anything but guess where the channel was. I guessed wrong. With a great grinding roar *Minots Light* rode up on the rocks, swung around, and came to rest with her rail and the end of the main boom in the water.

We got the sails down and a   173

Nights at anchor are part
of the pleasure of
cruising. Top: Minots Light
in Adriatic harbor.
Left: Rafted together for a
gam. Right: Anchor
carried on deck is big help
in boat of fair size.

friendly Swede in an outboard boat apologized for the absence of the buoy and took an anchor off in the direction of the channel. Five people cranking on three winches squeezed the anchor rode to a fraction of its normal diameter, but we didn't budge. Then a spectator in a converted fishing boat took a 300-foot line attached to our spinnaker halyard and was able to heel us further until we slid off. At one point the cabin side was awash; it must have been a remarkable sight. An inspection showed no damage to the rig and no water in the bilge. We carefully followed a local boat through the unmarked channel—for once local knowledge was right—and anchored in a secluded cove to kill a bottle of whiskey.

When *Minots Light* was hauled for winter storage the only signs of the grounding were three grooves an eighth of an inch deep in the iron keel. As far as I am concerned, there is nothing to beat a steel hull for sheer strength in a large yacht.

The attentive reader will have noticed no mention of having another vessel tow a stranded boat clear. Only in a very few special instances is this a good idea; the proper role for volunteer help is to take an anchor out. When there is no hurry involved, I believe the practical experience of getting oneself out of trouble without assistance is invaluable. It is nice to have done it, just as it is nice to have survived a gale at sea. The crew of a smallish sailboat can almost always free it without too much agony, and few passing craft are equal to the task of hauling off a large one that is hard aground.

A degree of mental strain is inseparable from the exercise of seamanship. The sailor who always assumes his anchor will hold and that, if it doesn't, somebody will be there to help him may escape gray hair for a long time, but all he is really doing is falling into a trap laid by that master confidence artist, the sea. I love the sea, but I don't trust it, and perhaps I enjoy its company the more for the battle of wits we engage in whenever I set out on a sail. To me, seamanship means keeping the stakes low enough so that even when I lose a round, I am happy to return for another.

Safety is another aspect of seamanship that deserves special note. Given care and good sense in its management, no

174

*Above: Caution is needed near
giant ships like this one since their
speeds are difficult to judge
and they cannot readily slow down
or change course. Maxim of
wise sailor is, "Big boat has
right of way." Left: To relax
vigilance is to invite catastrophe.*

means of transport is as safe as a sailboat, let alone as delightful. But Murphy's Law nevertheless applies: sooner or later everything that can happen, will happen.

Of the variety of mishaps that can occur on a sailboat, only three worry me to any real extent: falling overboard, being seriously injured, and being run down by a ship.

With a diesel rather than a gasoline engine, a carbon-dioxide fire-extinguishing system for the engine room plus hand extinguishers, and an automatically-inflating life raft, I feel reasonably secure against perishing from explosion, fire, and sinking. But even though I carry life rings with strobe lights and a full medical outfit (not just a first-aid kit), I am not sure how able my wife would be to recover me if I fell off *Minots Light* while sailing in a strong wind or how any of us would cope with somebody's fractured skull until we could get help or reach port. And before I had a radar installed in self-defense, I was regularly terrified by the inexcusably rotten seamanship of and disregard of the Rules of the Road by a significant proportion of those in charge of merchant ships at sea.

The most important step in coming to terms with the first two of these hazards is to be meticulous in guarding against them. Lifelines and pulpits are absolutely necessary on any sailboat venturing into open water. So are safety belts for all hands. On *Minots Light* safety belts are worn at night, in winds of more than moderate strength, in rough seas, and whenever else the skipper thinks they might be a good idea. Anybody who might object to wearing one would be returned immediately to shore to grow up, but the problem has not yet arisen. It is worth noting that more people have gone overboard from cockpits than from foredecks. A nylon line is secured from bow to stern on both sides of the boat so a man can go forward with his belt hooked on at all times. All sailing jackets are red or orange and contain built-in buoyancy, just in case. Booms are guyed forward on a run. Nobody stands near a boom when the halyard brake is released. Fending off is done with fenders, not with hands or feet except for dinghies. Horseplay on deck is forbidden, *forbudt, verboten, prohibido, interdit.* Obvious pre-

*After day on the water
needs of the vessel must be
attended to first. Then
crew can relax its discipline
and indulge its cravings,
whether to put on jacket and
tie, to have good wash, or
just to fool around.*

cautions, but effective if habitually applied.

The best practical analysis of how to deal with a man overboard, should it happen, appeared in the November 1970 issue of the British magazine *Yachting Monthly*. Every sailor should read it. For injuries and illness at sea, the wisest thing to do, apart from carrying a doctor on board, would seem to be to take a collection of "First Aid at Sea" books and pamphlets (each covers slightly different ground and multiple opinions are useful), the various items they suggest, a copy of *The Merck Manual of Diagnosis and Therapy,* and perhaps a textbook of minor surgery.

Collisions can occur on any body of water, from the smallest inland lake to the vastest ocean. They constitute a more and more serious problem as the number of boats in use and their average speeds both increase.

The relative slowness of a sailboat makes it a natural victim, and lucky is the sailor whose heart does not stop a dozen times a season as a boat or ship cuts across his bow with only yards to spare. There is nevertheless much an alert helms-

man can do to avoid being struck. A loud blast of the horn may be enough to wake an inattentive skipper, or perhaps a flare at night. Unfortunately autopilots are deaf as well as blind, and it is prudent to try to get out of the way in good time if there is no sign of life at the wheel of an oncoming vessel.

Sailboats not infrequently have themselves to blame for collisions. The fashion for deck-sweeping genoas is particularly unfortunate in this respect, since a rather large blind spot to leeward is inevitable with such a sail. A sailor who uses low-cut genoas in busy waters without a proper lookout is in exactly the same category as a man who uses an autopilot in busy waters without a proper lookout—both of them belong permanently ashore.

Yachts are not the only offenders when it comes to careless operation. To be run down by a ship is not an especially rare event, and near misses are so common few bother to record them. The greatest external danger to a yacht in most coastal waters comes not from gales but from ships operated with criminal carelessness, sometimes even with deliberate malice. The

popular imagination pictures the bridge of a merchant ship as a chamber lined with instruments and populated by serious, sober men who are dedicated to the Rules of the Road, keep a continuous lookout, maintain a radar plot, and in general behave in a manner befitting their calling and their responsibilities. What nonsense! I don't doubt that passenger liners are run in this way, at least when open to public gaze, but the majority of ships are prosaic cargo carriers in charge of individuals who all too often heed neither common sense nor the Rules of the Road.

An extreme point of view? According to a recent study concerning vessels of five hundred tons or more that was carried out by the U.S. Naval Oceanographic Office, from 1958 to 1967 "approximately seven per cent of the world's fleet was involved in a collision during each of the five years specified. Judging by the apparent consistency with which collisions occur every year, the annual average thus provided could conceivably be used as a forecast for future years. ...It would mean that approximately one ship in every fifteen would be the victim of a collision in any given year. This is indeed a matter

of serious concern."

More recent statistics confirm that the one-in-fifteen per year collision rate is still continuing—three collisions between large ships take place on the average every single day somewhere in the world. They are not Acts of God. The Oceanographic Office goes on to pinpoint the reason for this appalling record: "Very few instances have been recorded in which a collision was not the result of some Rule [of the Road] violation."

Smaller commercial vessels—coasters, fishing boats, harbor craft of various kinds—have an even worse record, and are more dangerous to the yachtsman because they use the same inshore waters he does. No large ship has ever altered course to avoid *Minots Light* when we had the unquestioned right of way and were clearly visible from miles away, but at least such ships maintain steady courses and never go out of their way to play chicken with us. I accept the fact that large ships are steered by automatic pilot with an imperfect lookout, if any, and I keep away from them. The only realistic Rule of the Road for a yacht is: "Big boat has the right of way."

But small ships are another matter, especially in confined waters. Much more often than not their crews are decent men, helpful and friendly to the sailor even though not particularly respectful of the Rules of the Road. A minority are thugs who take pleasure in endangering yachts by their inexcusable antics. Every area has its nautical hoodlums: the tugs around New York which always seem to go past small boats at full speed a few yards away; the self-propelled barges of the Dutch canals which like to use yachts already made fast in a lock as fenders; the fishing boats of the Atlantic coast of France which are notorious for their attempts to ram yachts at sea. Fortunately, the skippers of the latter are usually too drunk to succeed. Six fishing boats, one after the other, tried to hit *Minots Light* off Audierne in Brittany, and only missed by a few feet. But evasive action does not always work. In August of 1970 the French trawler *Le Temps de Cerise* pursued the British yawl *Nicolette* on a clear day in the Bay of Biscay and despite the best efforts of *Nicolette* to stay clear succeeded in striking her amidships. Three people were killed as *Nicolette* went down.

What can the yachtsman do to avoid attacking ships? A fair amount, since sailboats are more maneuverable than ships. A good lookout is obviously essential. Automatic steering, whether by wind vane or under compass control, is a boon to the sailor who likes to cruise shorthanded, but it is tempting fate for him not to keep track of ships in his vicinity. Propeller shafts should never be locked in such a way that the helmsman cannot put the engine in gear in an emergency without leaving the cockpit. Some sort of device is needed to keep the shaft of a boat with a hydraulic gearbox from turning when under sail, but this can be a friction brake—perhaps a modified automobile brake—which the engine can override if necessary.

To keep the problem in perspective, I repeat that, on the whole, the sea is a safe place, and most vessels behave predictably if incorrectly. But as long as no official action is ever taken against rogue skippers regardless of how dangerous their actions are, they will remain, for me at least, the principal hazard of the sea. 181

San Francisco Bay, California

In Sheltered Waters

*Most sailing is done in sheltered waters, both salt
and fresh. Such waters are ideal
for day sailing and one-design racing, and quite frequently
limited cruising is also possible.
If the drama of the open sea is missing, there is
in exchange the ease with which
the sailor can go afloat whenever he feels like it.*

Lake Anywhere, U.S.A.

Newport Beach, California

Tinsley Island, California

Shrewsbury River, New Jersey

Cowes, England

Shelter is a relative term to the sailor, and strong
winds can bring problems anywhere.
But absence of really rough water and proximity of places
to tie up permit active sailing with
little expenditure of time or money. Catboats (left)
are vessels of charm and
character well suited for waters of limited depth.

Sailor's skills are always fun to
exercise, and setting of mountains or forest enhances
the pleasure. Dinghies are often
kept ashore when not in use, and launching them is
especially simple in tideless waters.

Lake Dillon, Colorado

Annapolis, Maryland

Lysekil, Sweden

Thousand Islands, New York

Pacific Northwest (right) is region
of extraordinary beauty with year-round mild climate.
Extensive cruising is possible
there without venturing into Pacific deeps.
Scows (below) are familiar
sight on larger lakes of Wisconsin and Minnesota.

Sausalito, California

Lake Mendota, Wisconsin

Puget Sound, Washington

10 Baltic

Reaches

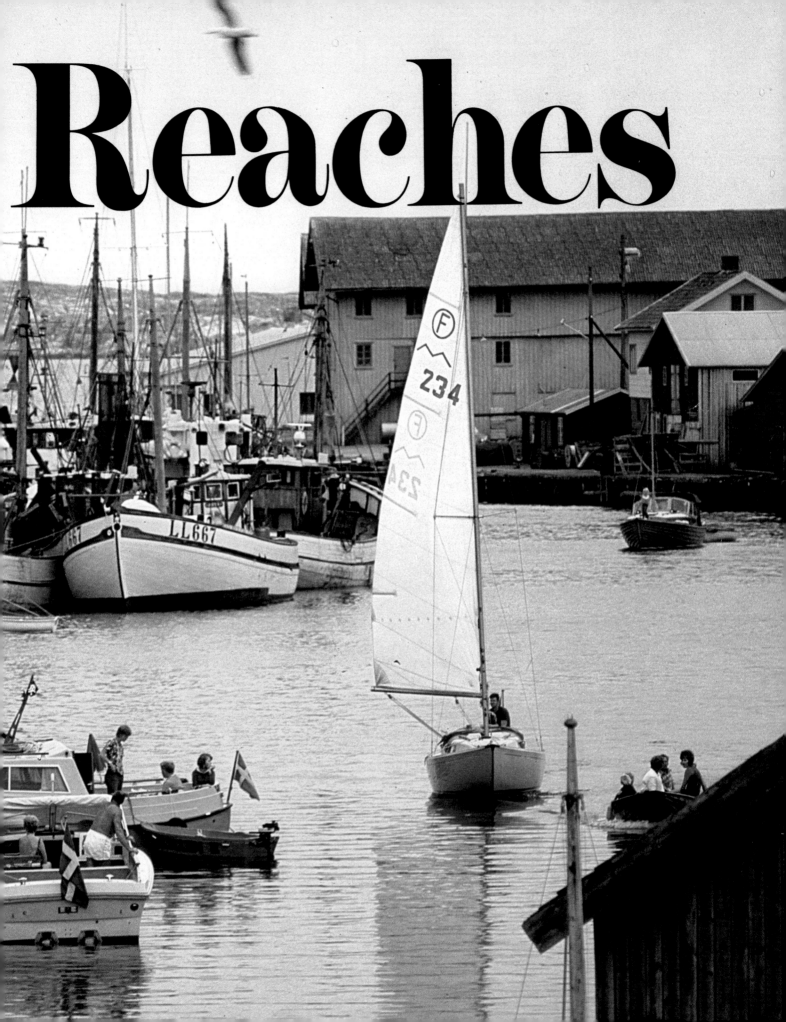

The Baltic Sea—by which I mean in particular the waters of the east coast of Sweden and of the south coast of Finland—is gentler and more feminine in character than Maine, more woodwind than brass, but it offers much the same rewards to the sailor. The scale is smaller. Most of the islands are tiny, the passages between them often narrow. The sea is hardly ever rough, and no tides complicate matters. But for all the intricacy of the detail, the canvas is huge, with tens of thousands of wooded islands scattered across hundreds of miles of blue, almost fresh water. The basic theme is everywhere the same, the variations endless. One could spend a lifetime sailing in the Baltic and never anchor twice in the same place.

The uncertain climate and remote location of the Baltic mean that the drones who fill every cranny of most of the world's yachting centers stay clear. Not only are visitors rare, but Swedes and Finns pour southward in migratory swarms every summer to leave their own paradise barely tenanted. (I appreciate their lust for reliable sunshine, as does anyone who has experienced the gloom of a Scandinavian winter.) As a result the Baltic is a haven for those able to celebrate nature in solitude.

Despite six cruises to the Baltic at this writing, their spell retains its hold, and next summer will once more see the black hull and red sails of *Minots Light* in the archipelagos of Sweden and Finland. I look forward to deriving sustenance again from the pines and birches of the islands, from the glitter of the waters, from the brooding silence of the long evenings.

The Baltic is not for everyone, and in writing about it I am not trying to lure anyone there. What I hope to do is to give some hint of why I am content to spend many of my summers in one region despite an ability to range much farther; of why rediscovery can be as vivid to the sailor as discovery. And, underlying everything else, of why I find cruising under sail an indispensable part of a full life.

Light airs are the rule in the Baltic in late spring and early summer. In an average year winds exceed ten knots only a

*Opening pages: Scandinavia might
have been designed for
the sailor, so much does it offer
him. Most harbors there are
small, like this one in Sweden, but
visiting boats are always
welcome. Expert handling under
sail is taken for granted.*

third of the time in May, June, and July, and gales are rare. As fall approaches, though, boisterous days become less exceptional and rail-down sailing joins the menu as a seasonal specialty.

The most sensible Baltic strategy is to make a counterclockwise circuit. Starting from Denmark fair winds are probable around the south and east coasts of Sweden and across the Åland archipelago to Finland. On the return, windward going is minimized by cutting across Sweden via the Göta Canal.

It is cold in May and early June in the Baltic, with air and water temperatures about what they are on the Maine coast at that time of year. Hardly any yachts are out cruising, and few summer houses are occupied except on sunny weekends. It is possible to sail for hours through the Swedish and Finnish archipelagos in spring without meeting another boat.

The air is cold and clear, the days are long and grow longer as one goes farther north. On deck gloved hands grip the wheel, a plume of smoke rises from the Charlie Noble of the cabin heater, overhead gulls squawk and starlings screech. A flash of movement in the open doorway of a cabin signals another member of this private universe. My wife reproaches me for desecrating the purity of the scene by inspecting the cabin through binoculars. I hand them to her; she sees the woman inside staring at us through her own pair. Everybody waves, and the cabin disappears as we follow the slalom course of the channel.

Only the mainsail and boomed forestaysail are up, for ease of maneuver. Going fast can be dangerous in these waters. Some stretches of intricate pilotage remind me of rapid-transit chess: ten seconds to make a move, no chance to think twice, keep calm or all is lost.

Finally it is 1830 and we have been under way for twelve hours, long enough. A cove to port beckons, the chart shows a mud bottom and sufficient depth. The rattle of the anchor chain running out shatters the air but does not disturb a duck and her clutch of fluffy offspring. We are tired, chilled, and hungry, ripe for hot mugs of Moose Milk. I put a slug each of rum, brandy, and whiskey into a pot with a large

193

gob of sweetened condensed milk, add some water, bring it all to a boil, and serve with cinnamon and nutmeg. None is left over.

As the Baltic summer matures, air and water warm up. Sweaters are stowed, hatches opened, the swimming ladder is dug out from the bottom of the sail locker. In a good year, such as 1969 was, the water up north is as inviting in July and August as it is in the Mediterranean.

But all years are not good years. In 1970 we had planned a cruise elsewhere, and we changed our minds at literally the last moment as memories of the previous year flocked back. Off we went to Finland once more, now to find cold, wet weather with stiff winds and lumpy seas the rule. There were some fine days, but not a great many, and worst of all the water temperature was usually too cold for bathing. In one anchorage near Hanko in mid-July the water was 46 degrees Fahrenheit, 20 degrees colder than it had been in the same place exactly a year before. It was still a worthwhile cruise without question, but we missed the swim before breakfast, the pierce of an iced beer on a hot

afternoon.

For a yacht coming from the English Channel the most convenient route to the Baltic makes use of the Kiel Canal, especially if the Dutch and German coasts are to be visited beforehand. The canal links Brunsbüttelkoog on the Elbe River with Holtenau on Kiel Bay, and there are locks at each end. The distance between locks is fifty-three miles, a day's run. It is necessary to time one's arrival off the mouth of the Elbe to assure a fair current all the way to Brunsbüttelkoog. There is a lot of difference between carrying a flood of two knots and fighting an ebb of three knots.

The canal trip is interesting and undemanding. There is always something to look at, ships of all kinds and nationalities and a few pretty stretches of countryside. The speed limit is 15 kilometers per hour, which is about 8 knots. Proceeding under sail alone is forbidden, but it is all right to motorsail at a minimum speed of 6 kilometers per hour (3¼ knots); the winds are usually so fluky that nearly all yachts use power only. Signs on shore mark every half kilometer, making it easy to calibrate speed-and-distance logs. There are four official stopping

Absence of tide makes it easy to tie
up in Baltic. Below left:
Visiting yachts in Vadstena, Sweden;
right: Langelinie harbor,
Copenhagen, is always full, but
there is usually room for
one more. Bottom: Kiel Canal provides
convenient access to Baltic.

places for yachts in the canal, plus small basins at each end.

One can spend a whole summer just in Danish waters and have a very fine time; more than one summer, in fact. But I prefer to think of Denmark as appetizer and dessert, with the archipelagos of the Baltic as the main course.

Almost any course through the Danish islands is rewarding. There are few good anchorages but innumerable man-made harbors where one can tie up alongside in security. There is no tide, though the water level may change by a few feet from time to time depending on the wind direction and strength. Picturesque towns such as Aerøskøping are in all the guidebooks and tend to be crowded as a result. The sailor is better off to ignore conventional tourist literature and to go where the wind takes him. I never saw mention of Fejø in the Smaalands Farvandet south of Sjaelland, or of Sejerø near Kalundborg, or even of the astonishing island of Anholt in the Kattegat before going to them, and I prefer any of them to Aerøskøping.

I visit Anholt every summer I am in the Baltic. Only two hundred people live there, nearly all well inland in a small village sheltered from the winter winds. Fishing is the only industry. The island is four-fifths desert, not wholly bare but patched with tall grass and scrub growth of various kinds.

The harbor of Anholt is excellent and well protected by a series of breakwaters. Usually there is room for yachts to lie alongside a wooden pier that is part of the inner breakwater; if not, an anchor can be dropped astern and the bow secured to the pier. The bottom provides good holding. Fresh fish can be obtained at the fishhouse on the quay, and provisions come in daily to the little shop there.

Anholt is ringed by miles of fine beach with almost nobody to make use of it. The only visitors are a few yachtsmen and a few campers—there are no day-trippers and no hotels. Past the immediate vicinity of the harbor, people space themselves out along the beach, and bathing suits disappear. One can walk for hours along unbroken beach, stopping now and then for a swim, a snack, a sunbath. Or one can simply sit back in a hollow in the nearby dunes to watch a distant

196

sailboat as it creeps slowly closer.

To me, a few days at Anholt form a perfect interlude in a Scandinavian cruise. Anholt can be enjoyed without effort and left without regret, a good place to sort out memories of what went before and to work up steam for what is to come. I wish there were more Anholts.

Every visitor to Denmark eventually ends up in Copenhagen. It is my favorite city anywhere. To hear it called the Paris of the North infuriates me (as it does the Danes, too), for I have lived in both places and they simply have nothing in common apart from an appreciation of good food and drink. One need only compare Tivoli with the Tuileries, or the open face of a Copenhagen girl with the tight, sour mask of a Parisienne to see the difference in style between the two cities. I felt at home in Copenhagen the first day I arrived. Four years of living in Paris have convinced me that nobody, nobody at all, feels truly at home there.

Bound east from Copenhagen time is saved by passing through the Falsterbo Canal at the southwest corner of Sweden. There is one long lock, so long that one does not stop inside it but continues going as the gate astern closes and the gate ahead opens. The south coast of Sweden is of no interest, though a number of commercial ports there are useful for overnight stops. It is far more fun to make for one of the harbors on the Danish island of Bornholm or, still better, for its neighbor Christiansø.

Just north of Kråkelund on Sweden's east coast islands begin to appear in profusion, and from then on it is possible to sail among them in sheltered waters most of the way to Stockholm. In my opinion this region is prettier and more interesting than the more famous Stockholm archipelago. Thin lines on the Swedish charts indicate recommended routes and tiny anchors mark suggested anchorages, but the vessels the cartographer has in mind are coasters and often other routes and anchorages will prove more rewarding.

Instead of following the coast, one can stay offshore and stop at Visby on the island of Gotland. Visby reached its zenith seven hundred years ago, when it was the leading commercial center of northern Europe. Today it is one of the leading tourist

One-design racing
is passion in Scandinavia.
Opposite: 505's near
Lysekil, Sweden. Above:
Knarrs, popular in
Denmark, can also be
used for limited
cruising. Left: Stern
view of Paul Elvstrøm
is more familiar
to his competitors.

traps of northern Europe and bearable only very early and late in the season.

No city is so well situated for the sailor as Stockholm, with an immense and beautiful archipelago spread out before it. And the Swedes make good use of it, with thousands of yachts out sailing on nice weekends. Large areas of the archipelago have been only sketchily surveyed and hazards there have been left unmarked, which doesn't seem to deter local yachtsmen, but strangers should be careful there. However, there is such a variety of marked channels that a visitor has little reason to stray from them. Foreign yachts often tie up at the quay alongside Strandvagen in the middle of Stockholm, but this is a noisy, excessively public place made worse by the wash of passing ships. I prefer one of the marinas just outside the city, for example the one at Djurgården.

Finland is at the eastern end of the Baltic. Off its lovely, lonely coast lie islands by the tens of thousands, wooded islands that show little of the hand of man. I write about Finland with some reluctance, because there seem to be few yachts there relative to the extent of its waters and I would like to see this happy situation continue. Fantsnäs is a small peninsula near Lovisa, a day's sail east of Helsinki. My friend Johan, who is a Finn by birth but who has lived in America for forty years, has a summer house at Fantsnäs where he spends a few months each year. One winter's night in New York he told me about Fantsnäs and the archipelago around it, a warren of islands he has sailed in since he was a boy. "You must go there," he said. But Fantsnäs is many thousands of miles from New York, and within a week his injunction had vanished into that recess of my mind where daydreams dwell.

Each year at Christmas we make our plans for the coming summer's cruising. In 1963 we had sailed *Minots Light* to Scotland and on to the Baltic via the Caledonian and Göta canals, and in September we had made our way south and west to Denmark where we were spending the winter. Now, at year's end, the living room of our rented house near Elsinore was carpeted with charts and dividers marched across Europe. Somehow, as we debated this destination and that, Johan's words returned. And so it was decided: Finland it would be.

The cold half-light of the Danish winter gradually gave way to the warm sun of spring. Early in May *Minots Light* slid back into the Kattegat from Molich's yard at Hundested, and with a few weeks of fitting out and provisioning she was ready to go. We left Denmark in June and in a few days were on Sweden's east coast headed for Stockholm. Our course lay among hundreds of islands, large and small, rocky and green, deserted and decked with painted houses. Day followed day of sunshine, and the clear Baltic twinkled as we ran before mild southwesterly breezes.

Five easy sailing days took us from Stockholm to Helsinki. There Johan's cousin Gösta joined us as pilot, and we were grateful for his presence because the last part of the trip to Fantsnäs involves an intricate passage past unbuoyed and largely uncharted underwater hazards. Fantsnäs turned out to be even more magical than Johan had intimated, and we have returned there regularly in the years since.

No account of cruising in Finland is complete without mention of the sauna, a source of health and pleasure whose attractions baffle the uninitiated but which is practically a religion with the Finns.

A typical sauna (the word applies both to the experience and to the chamber it takes place in) is a small wooden building on the shore of a lake or the sea. In one corner is a furnace, traditionally wood-burning but often run by electricity these days. A heap of stones rests on the furnace. Across the room are two wooden platforms, one above the other, on which the bathers sit or lie. The sauna is preheated to perhaps 200 degrees Fahrenheit, sometimes more, and a blast of heat greets the bather on entering. Novices and weaklings go to the lower platform, heroes to the upper one.

Though I am now an old hand at taking saunas, and am just as addicted to them as any Finn, the first few minutes are always a bit of an ordeal. But just in time heavy perspiration starts, and the initial agony changes to a feeling of deep relaxation.

After a while the bathers beat each other with whisks of birch branches to stimulate the circulation, and some joker may throw a handful of water on the hot

201

*Opposite & bottom:
Göta Canal route
across Sweden involves 64
locks and 214 miles
of beautiful lakes and
countryside. Left
& below: Double-enders are
common in Scandinavia.*

stones to produce a momentary surge of superheated steam. This is as close to hell as I want to come. Next comes a thorough scrubbing in an antechamber, with the bathers customarily washing each other's backs. After rinsing the soap off, one may or may not return to the sauna itself for a few minutes.

At this point comes the Cooling Off in which the bather plunges into a nearby body of water (or rolls in the snow if it's winter) to produce a bracing shock. Wham! Instantly the years fall away and one is young and alive again, supple as a birch sapling and full of new-found vigor.

Now back to the sauna for another round to complete the job of renewing body and soul. Finally, after a total of an hour or so, the sauna is over, and the bathers sit together on the porch to drink beer and listen to the whisper of the pine trees and the calls of distant birds.

A bonus awarded those who journey all the way to Finland is the excellence of Finnish charts and sea marks. The pains taken with them come as a relief after a passage through Swedish waters, where marks are often so poorly placed that it is difficult to find the entrances to certain tricky passages, buoys shown on an up-to-date chart are missing all season, and other buoys not on the chart appear mysteriously in one's path. I write with passion because I have three times been set aground on rocks by the vagaries of the Swedish buoyage. In 1970 we even found a whole lighthouse west of Landsort that was not on a new chart dated 1970 and corrected (so it said) to include all marks to be installed in that year.

On the other hand, pilotage in Finland is a pleasure. An especially appreciated gesture of their cartographers is to state the controlling depth of every route. These depths are checked periodically by drags—I have seen this being done—and are very conservative: my depth sounder has never yet registered less than 12 feet in a 2.4-meter (7-feet, 10-inch) channel.

There is a handy mnemonic for Finnish buoys. A nordprick (north mark) that indicates a hazard to its north is in the form of a red down-pointing cone. This is a "northern lady," with the cone representing the glass of schnapps such a lady often has in her hand. A sydprick that indicates a hazard to its south is a black up-pointing cone— a "southern lady" with a wide skirt. A väst-prick is a pair of red cones with their points together—a "western lady" with a wasp waist. And an ostprick is a pair of black cones with their bases together—an "eastern lady" of substantial girth.

Returning to the west from the Baltic, a passage through the Göta Canal makes great sense. The canal starts at Mem, south of Stockholm, and terminates 214 miles and sixty-four locks later at Göteborg on Sweden's west coast. Only part of the route consists of man-made channels; included is a stretch of the Göta River and a number of lakes, some of them small and charming and others—Vättern and Vänern—that are virtually inland seas.

The prevailing summer breezes in Scandinavia are southwesterly, giving fair winds from Copenhagen round the south coast of Sweden and up its east coast. On the way back, the canal thus saves a probable slog to windward and also offers a restful interlude before open water is tackled again. The east-to-west crossing of the Göta Canal has two other advantages over a passage the other way. Boats are required to make fast to the south side of each lock, hence a westward passage means going alongside portside-to, which is the easy way in a single-screw vessel with a right-hand propeller. With sixty-four locks in all, even on a boat smaller than *Minots Light,* the difference in handling ease adds up. Finally, the swift current in the Göta River provides a fast run downstream, a frustratingly slow one upstream.

Most of the Göta Canal locks are little different from what they were when they were built a century and a half ago. Thus one is able to re-create to some extent nineteenth-century canal life, not only in Sweden but elsewhere in Europe and in America where canals like this flourished before the railways came. The canal is owned by a private company, and dues depend on the size of the boat. Recently it cost a total of $95 for *Minots Light,* 58 feet overall, to go through, and $42 for *Shenandoah,* a 15-foot sloop belonging to my children which we towed most of the way. These charges are modest in view of what is offered.

Nearly all the locks are oper-

Above: Barren islands near Smögen on Sweden's west coast. Above right: Smögen harbor. Right: Minots Light *and* Indigo *tied to shore south of Stockholm. Far right: Uncrowded anchorages are easy to find in Baltic.*

ated by hand, and each yacht is supposed to furnish a person to help the lockkeeper close and open the gates and sluices. It sounds like work but is such fun that passersby often pitch in to help. Two people are needed on board to tend bow and stern lines, simple enough on a small boat but calling for good judgment and strong arms (or winches) on a large one as water boils into the lock when ascending. Plenty of fenders are required: we use fourteen on *Minots Light,* and Swedish yachts often have sacks of wood shavings to supplement their regular fenders.

The speed limit in the canal is 4.8 knots, which gives plenty of time to enjoy the "soft curves of the canal's dreamy path through the umbrageous landscape," as the canal company's brochure puts it, not inaccurately. We usually take a week to go from Mem to Göteborg or vice-versa. There are scores of places to tie up for the night, plus the lakes where one can anchor in agreeable surroundings and go for a swim in good weather. Söderköping and Motala are especially convenient for shopping. In Vadstena, on Lake Vättern, there is a fine sixteenth-century castle worth visiting. Of the various routes possible across Lake Vänern, I like best the intricate but rewarding one that goes past the splendid castle of Läckö.

Canal traffic is light, but one must watch out for boats going the other way in some of the narrow, winding stretches near Forsvik. Here trees lean over the canal, and we usually break off a few branches with our rigging as we go past. Most canal users are small yachts, but there are several tourist steamers and an occasional small commercial vessel.

A visitor to the Baltic who returns via the Göta Canal has three routes before him for his re-entry to the North Sea —unless he has been so captivated that he leaves his boat in one of the excellent Scandinavian yards for another season there the following year. One of these routes is the Kiel Canal, another is Limfjord, and the third is the Skagerrak.

Limfjord is not a fjord in the Norwegian sense but an irregular, shallow body of water that meanders across the northern end of Jutland. It is bordered by farmland and low, wooded hills, and, unusual for Denmark, there are many anchorages where some privacy is possible. I find Limfjord insipid and I am maddened by the stares of the cattle that line its shores; but its placidness will be a welcome memory while crossing the treacherous North Sea.

Southern Norway and the adjacent Bohuslan coast of Sweden have as their dominant scenic theme bare gray rock, softened here and there with outcrops of green where vegetation has somehow taken hold. It is all a bit too austere for my taste, though I acknowledge the friendliness of the inhabitants and the fine fish in the markets. A few of the harbors—notably Risör, Arendal, Lillesand—are certainly worth visiting if one is passing by, and Oslo is an interesting city. To me this coast is not a place to linger but to pass through on the way to or from Scotland or the fjord country to the north.

The west coast of Norway is a thousand miles of rugged mountains and spectacular fjords. A magnificent coast, justly famous, but a difficult one for the sailor. Anchoring is a problem because the water is usually deep right up to the shore, and few places have provision for yachts to tie up except temporarily. Winds tend to be too weak or too strong, rain is frequent, and the climate is raw even in midsummer. But the landscape *is* remarkable.

The influence of the Gulf Stream makes it entirely possible to cruise past the Arctic Circle to the Lofoten Islands and even farther to North Cape, the northernmost point of Europe, a harsh, empty, somber region that has a strong appeal to some temperaments. It is a serious part of the world, no place to be caught with inadequate gear or crew, but the more rewarding for that reason. The Maelstrom of Norse mythology and Poe's story lies up that way, actually a pair of tidal races called Moskenström and Saltström today.

Clearly, Scandinavia has plenty to offer the cruising sailor. But it is not variety that continues to attract me there, and certainly not reliable weather. I simply am at peace with myself sailing in the Baltic, just as I was on the Maine coast. Other sailors experience similar feelings of belonging in a certain part of the world at the helm of their vessels. There are few deeper satisfactions than such a discovery of one's natural home, wherever it may be.

lands

very island has a personality of its own. The more remote the island, the less it resembles anywhere else. Even today, to set out across blue water for an unfamiliar island is to recapture some of that sense of eager anticipation of surprise that possessed the explorers of long ago. A sailboat in a mainland harbor always seems out of place to me, a caged bird of passage impatiently awaiting its freedom. An island is a more appropriate habitat, perhaps because a sailboat is a self-sufficient island in itself. When I visit an island by ferry or by airplane I am a stranger, an alien presence deposited there arbitrarily and soon to be plucked away leaving no trace. But when I arrive under sail I feel part of the scene at once, a distant cousin back to renew family ties.

I remember strolling along the Quai Bir-Hakeim in Papeete one morning when a small white ketch entered the harbor. She looked a mess to me, and I would not have cared to cross an inland lake in her, much less to sail from New Zealand to Tahiti.

Her paint was discolored and peeling, her rigging rusty, her cordage frayed—a sad spectacle. Nobody but me seemed to care about her ratty state. Within moments of tying up, a small crowd of jovial Tahitians was welcoming the crew of the ketch, and by that evening three girls had moved on board, baskets of fruit had been hung underneath the awning, and a community sing was in progress in the cockpit. I had come by air, and felt throughout my entire stay as though a pane of glass lay between me and the life of the island.

Islands far afield are a perpetual lure. Innumerable sailors have pointed the prows of their white-winged vessels toward the South Pacific, the West Indies, and the eastern Mediterranean in search of the perfect island. Once found, such an island becomes part of the sailor and he part of it.

The Pacific islands have a unique grip on the sailor's imagination, though he may well find it more practical to settle for islands nearer home. None of the many people I know who have cruised in the South Pacific has regretted the experience, despite the thousands of miles of sailing needed to get there plus the long slog back. I spent an afternoon with Bernard Moitessier before he embarked on his nonstop single-handed circumnavigation, and such were his reminiscences of the Pacific that I was not surprised when, after completing a circuit of the Southern Ocean, he continued on for another half lap to Tahiti instead of returning to Europe to claim the kudos that certainly should have been his due.

The opulent sights, sounds, and smells of Polynesia account for only part of its magnetism. I will not repeat the centuries-old clichés about its inhabitants, but I will say that whenever I came upon a group of people on a palm-fringed beach in Samoa or Tahiti I had no trouble in picturing them planning a voyage to be guided only by the stars and the swells of the sea as their ancestors had been, thousands of years before Europeans dared to venture in those trackless waters.

Islands nearer home may also possess distinctive atmospheres. Nantucket is an example, and its moors, surf-washed beaches, and austere frame houses retain their charm despite hordes of summer people. I like the smell of the sea in Nantucket, and the way both sunshine and fog seem equally appropriate there.

Martha's Vineyard and the Elizabeth Islands nearby are also attractive, though lacking the sense of remoteness that pervades Nantucket. Distances are not great in this area, but strong tides and an abundance of off-lying shoals present interesting exercises in pilotage, particularly in thick weather or at night. There is no better classroom for learning to cruise than the waters south of Cape Cod, where carrots in the form of fine harbors abound for the novice and there are just enough sticks in wait to discourage carelessness. A passage from Woods Hole or Vineyard Haven to Cuttyhunk against the usual afternoon southwesterly is a long step toward a diploma in sailing to windward, and then to beat through the narrow channel into Cuttyhunk's miniature harbor and anchor in the thicket of boats there without using the engine might well be part of a final exam in seamanship. (But I would be inclined to give an equal grade for a refusal to undertake something so foolhardy except in a very small boat. My hands shook

213

*Clockwise from
upper left: St. Thomas,
Virgin Islands;
anchorage in
Society Islands of
Polynesia; Caneel Bay,
Virgin Islands;
Finnish archipelago
east of Helsinki;
Walker's Cay, Bahamas;
harbor of Baltic
island of Christiansø.*

215

for an hour afterward the last time I did it.)

Maine, of course, is where islands have been strewn with a lavish hand for the benefit of the sailor. Every visitor has his own favorite, and I would not argue with someone who has lost his heart to Roque Island or Matinicus. If forced to make a choice, I would probably pick Isle au Haut. I have never had to share an anchorage in Isle au Haut, and few houses or roads punctuate its high wooded slopes. Which is as well, because although some of the whaling flavor of Nantucket has managed to survive, I doubt that one could look at Isle au Haut as though with the eyes of Champlain, or conceivably of Leif Ericsson, were it littered with cars, hot-dog stands, and junk shops.

Still, distance acts as a prism to expand perception. The islands that have fascinated me most are all abroad. The rugged topography, devotion to fishing, and presence of a small summer colony make Christiansø in the Baltic reminiscent of a Maine island, but a visit there has a different, stronger flavor. A Scandinavian sailor touring Maine would probably say the same thing in reverse.

Christiansø is a speck of rock belonging to Denmark that lies south of Sweden near Bornholm. It is separated by a narrow strait from an even smaller island, Frederiksø. The strait is the harbor, used for hundreds of years by warships and more recently by a few fishing boats, the daily ferry, and an occasional yacht. A rickety bridge joins the islands and can be swung aside to permit a boat to pass through. Perhaps a hundred and fifty people live here permanently, mostly fishermen and their families but also a few craftsmen, teachers, and lighthouse keepers.

Contrasts abound in Christiansø. The military past of the island is evident in its ring of seventeenth-century fortifications, ancient cannon still in place, and neat stacks of cannonballs, but the atmosphere is one of deep peace. The year-round residents live in two facing rows of buildings that once were barracks. The summer people have tiny stone houses, each a miniature fortress set in a handkerchief of walled garden and tucked away in the irregular landscape almost out of sight of its neighbors. So barren is the island that all the soil for its gardens had to be brought from Bornholm, a dozen miles away. The houses are all owned by the government, and to be able to rent one is a sought-after privilege. Paths twist in and out, and each turning brings an unexpected vista: a flash of sea, a flood of golden blossoms, a giant anchor from long ago, a heroic bust of a bearded man (who? why?), a naked sunbather who thinks she is concealed—or does she?

The islands of the Mediterranean are in an entirely different category from the tropical ones of the Pacific and Caribbean, not to mention those of New England and the Baltic, not only in physical character but also in their historical significance and style of life.

Each time I sail in the cobalt-blue Mediterranean I feel younger and more alive despite the enervating heat, better disposed toward my fellow men despite instances of unreliability which seem to occur there more often than elsewhere, and even better fed despite the intrinsic monotony of a cuisine based on olive oil, garlic, and coarse wine. Perhaps it is the extraordinarily wide sweep of sky that accounts for the en-

chantment of the Mediterranean, or perhaps the timeless quality of life there, with each day hardly distinguishable from the one before or the one after. Intellectually and emotionally I am drawn elsewhere, but my body finds the ease of the Mediterranean far more to its liking, and I find it advisable to yield to its cravings from time to time.

It is an old story that there is either not enough wind in the Mediterranean or far too much. On the whole this is a fair summary of the situation. Weeks can go by with only faint breezes barely enough to move a sailboat, then without warning a mistral or tramontana or bora or sirocco can strike. There is nothing remarkable about motoring for several hundred miles over a rippleless sea of glass in the Med, though land and sea breezes are common near most coastlines. The gales pack a wallop, and may extend well beyond their normal haunts. One midnight a 60-knot mistral came to whip into white foam the harbor of Fornells on Menorca, two hundred miles from the Rhône Valley where it originated. All around yachts were dragging their anchors and finding it impossible to motor upwind to reset them in

217

*Coasts of Maine (above), Cape Cod
(right), and southern France (opposite)
are doubly blessed, being attractive
in themselves and having inviting islands
within easy reach. The more
remote an island, the greater its
appeal, but every island has
unique character that rewards a visit.*

the lee of the land; our anchor held with the help of the engine to ease the strain, and when we left a few days later we found it was quite a project to retrieve the deeply buried Danforth.

Still, fine sailing days do turn up regularly, and it is part of the magic of the Mediterranean that such days seem to sparkle in the memory more than similar days elsewhere. We once carried an amiable southwesterly breeze from Palma de Mallorca to Puerto Andraitx on a brilliant morning amid splashes of warm spray that set bronzed skin tingling, there to anchor near the outer breakwater and, following a swim, to go ashore for a paella in the cool interior of a restaurant, and finally, after a siesta in the shade of the awnings, to ghost back to Palma in a dying wind with all the light sails up and the floodlit Bellver Castle adrift in the sky to port. A trip so ordinary as to be banal, hardly worth noting in the log, but forever after a golden thread in the fabric of one's existence.

The Mediterranean in summer can be very hot. Awnings for the entire boat are essential, not just for the cockpit, and de-tachable side curtains are a good idea to intercept the low rays of the afternoon sun. Many owners of single-planked boats hang curtains around the topsides from rail to waterline to prevent seams from opening up.

A wind sail can be a lifesaver: this is a large vertical tube of cotton or Dacron eight or ten feet long, shaped roughly like a smoker's pipe. The mouthpiece (so to speak) is a snug fit in the forward hatch to which it is tied, and the other end, which has a wide funnel-like horizontal opening, is hoisted on a halyard and oriented to catch whatever breeze there is. Hoops every few feet keep the tube from collapsing. Even when there is no perceptible movement of air at deck level, a wind sail seems to scoop up zephyrs that make all the difference down below. Sluicing the decks with water at frequent intervals is also a help in surviving the heat. If one is planning a boat to be used in the Mediterranean, hatches should be made to hinge both fore and aft, all ports should open, and each Dorade vent should have two cowl positions, one directly over the deck pipe for better air flow as well as the usual one offset to keep water out.

The contrast between islands and an adjacent mainland is nowhere greater than in the Mediterranean. With few exceptions the mainland waterfronts are crowded, noisy, and dirty, often with a major road running along the quay and always with a mob of passersby day and night. Seldom is there any possibility of anchoring clear of the racket yet in sheltered water.

Yachts moored in such harbors seldom leave their berths despite the absence of peace and privacy. Their chief purpose is to serve as symbols of affluence, their secondary ones are to act as floating bars, as weekend cottages, as places to entertain *petites amies*. This is true to some extent for all yachts, of course, and is completely in keeping with the noblest traditions of the sport, but to an active sailor the atmosphere is not altogether sympathetic. The larger yachts always fly Liberian or Panamanian flags to avoid the attentions of the tax collector; I fly the standard American flag in the Mediterranean instead of the yacht ensign because the latter was always being mistaken for the flag of some obscure principality.

New marinas have appeared that modify this unappetizing picture, in particular a large number on the French coast, and civilized towns such as Alicante and Menton have their adherents. But to tour the Mediterranean by going from harbor to harbor around its rim is to miss the real treasures of that sea, which are its islands.

The Greek islands of the Ionian and Aegean seas, though full of interest, lack some element which I can't quite define, and they leave me unsatisfied. I find the islands off the Dalmatian coast of Yugoslavia (though not the coast itself) much more to my liking; they stand side by side with the archipelagos of Finland in my affection. From Mljet, Korčula, and Hvar in the south to Rab, Lošinj, and Krk (pronounced Krk) in the north, nearly every island has an ancient town worth a visit and a cove or two somewhere on its perimeter with herb-scented air, limpid water, and nobody there to break the spell that falls as soon as the anchor is down.

It is not necessary to go as far as Greece or Yugoslavia to find attractive islands in the Mediterranean, nor to stay out the night or two needed to reach the Balearics. Just off the French coast between Toulon

*Opposite: Corsica and Elba
are easy day's sail from Italian yacht
center of Portofino. Below
left: Port-Man is attractive harbor on
Mediterranean island of Port-Cros.
Below right: All Pacific wanderers stop in
Tahiti, and few are disappointed.
Botton: Ketch Aries in Aegean Sea.*

223

and Saint-Tropez, for instance, lie the small Îles d'Hyères. Why these islands are not overwhelmed with boats and people I do not know, because they are nicer than any other part of the Côte d'Azur. I spent three slothful weeks in the Îles d'Hyères one August, and though they were far from deserted, there was never any feeling of overcrowding except on the weekends.

Porquerolles, the westernmost of the Îles d'Hyères, has a sheltered harbor with good holding ground and a new marina. The village has shops and restaurants, and nearby are several beaches which shoal-draft boats can anchor off. During the week Porquerolles has a relaxed atmosphere and a walk through its tree-shaded interior is a pleasant way to escape the heat.

The beauty of the middle island, Port-Cros, has been celebrated in French literature beginning with Rabelais, and that beauty remains today. The *Guide Michelin* considers Port-Cros to be "un veritable Eden." I agree. Thinly populated, with camping forbidden and little in the way of tourist accommodations, Port-Cros is a garden alive with color and scent.

The island has two harbors, Port-Cros on the west and Port-Man on the east. Port-Cros has an exposed anchorage and the settlement there has little to offer. I am prejudiced against Port-Cros because late one night an ancient English gaff ketch dragged its anchor there in a westerly wind, and I awoke to the twang of the shrouds as the bowsprit of the ketch caught in them.

Port-Man provides better shelter, a perfect setting, and nothing man-made except one inconspicuous house (unoccupied when I was there) and a ruined stone tower. We sailed in under main alone early one morning, rounded up and dropped the anchor near the western shore. The main came down, and I dived overboard to check that the anchor had a secure grip on the sandy bottom and was not merely snagged in weed. Then I rowed in with the rubber dinghy to make fast a light nylon line to a projecting rock for added security. Only a bobble remained as legacy of the strong easterly that the day before had chased the weak-stomached away, and now fewer than a dozen yachts shared the harbor. We had breakfast in the cockpit listening to crickets chirping, the splashes of bathers, birds calling one another, the myriad rustles of a forest coming alive with the morning breeze.

Following coffee the awnings were rigged, which my wife and I decided was enough work for a while. The rest of that day and the two days following are blank in the log. I have vague memories of being visited by some Belgians and of later swimming over to their yawl to compare their rum punch with ours. We went for a walk in the forest as far as the Valley of Solitude, and on our return had a long swim to unkink our leg muscles after this unaccustomed exertion. Once in a while a boat would sail in, usually a small sloop with the turtle-like profile then coming into fashion. One of them tied up alongside and the skipper borrowed a wrench to fix his outboard. His crew of two bikini'd girls peeled potatoes and cleaned fish as he vainly tried to coax life into the motor. When dinner was ready he gave up and let the boat drift some distance away from us before anchoring.

Another little boat went boldly in toward a crevice in the shore. An anchor cast from the stern caught just in time, and in moments the bow nestled in the grass held by a line led to a tree. Two other boats of the same class followed and the three white transoms looked like eggs in a nest in the fading light. The stone tower opposite relinquished the sun last, and we slipped into the warm water for a last bathe before dinner.

A short distance from Port-Man is the Île du Levant, which thousands of cheerful nudists share with an outpost of the French navy. I had always read that nudist colonies are sober, earnest, puritanical places. Well, maybe so elsewhere, but the Île du Levant is quite the opposite, and many yachts anchor off its little beach to join the fun. Soon after we arrived there two naked girls swam out to say hello. "What a nice boat," said one of them. I agreed. "Are you alone?" asked the other. My wife sat up and said, firmly, "No, he is not." We chatted for a few minutes while they rested and then they swam over to a nearby trimaran. I gather they found whatever it was they were looking for on the trimaran, because they were soon on board and later waved happily to us as we went by in the dinghy on our way toward the beach.

12/Ocean

Passage

An ocean passage is every sailor's dream. For some, the dream is urgent and compelling and must be made into reality. For others, it is more of a daydream to flirt with, a vision to savor. But whether as a goal for action or as a goal for contemplation, to cross an ocean under sail has a unique symbolic significance for sailors everywhere. It is not hard to see why an ocean passage grips the imagination so strongly. To spend several weeks with only the wind for propulsion, the earth's magnetism for guidance, and the heavenly bodies to establish position on a featureless sea is to achieve a harmony with nature rare in the modern world.

One does not embark on an ocean voyage in a sailboat merely to get to the other side, any more than one climbs a mountain because it is there. What one seeks, consciously or not, is a deluge of sensations: sensations of pleasure and pain, of boredom and excitement, of humility and triumph, of terror and tranquility, sensations that follow one another in a headlong rush for weeks on end. It is an adventure of the spirit as much as of the body, one of the few truly profound experiences available in an age of triviality.

The preceding lines read strangely in these coldly rational times. But if it were not to satisfy a deep psychic need, why would anyone expose himself to certain discomfort and possible danger, not to mention extraordinary expense, in order to cover each day a third the distance an airplane overhead covers in an hour?

Little other than the regular use of sextant and chronometer is peculiar to the mechanics of an offshore voyage—the routine of a watch follows the same pattern a dozen and a thousand miles from land. But even though the individual differences are largely of degree, not of kind, ocean sailing is quite distinct from coastal passagemaking. One reason is the vast distances involved, so that the ship must be kept moving in the right direction without letup. Another is the isolation of ship and crew, which are wholly dependent on their own resources whatever the eventuality.

As far back as I can remember, I knew that sooner or later I would sail across the Atlantic in command of my own vessel. How and when were mere details. Eventually the time came when I had the right boat and the right wife, and thereupon it seemed the most natural thing in the world to undertake such a voyage.

At the time we left I had owned *Minots Light,* my fourth boat, for a little over two years. The first season had been spent mainly in cruising Down East, with some racing on Long Island Sound during spring and fall weekends. As a result I had a fairly clear idea of what changes were needed, and that winter a lot of work was done to bring *Minots Light* closer to being the proper yacht. The following summer went much more smoothly as a result, and with another winter to take care of odds and ends that were still outstanding, plus some new sails, *Minots Light* was in good shape for a serious voyage.

We were seven in all: Dixon and Ellen Long, Steve Zoll, Perry Lewis, Randy Taylor, my wife Germaine, and myself. None of us had previously spent more than one or two nights offshore at a time except Dixon, who had sailed from Japan to the West Indies in a 45-foot yawl and also had made a number of passages between New England and Saint Thomas.

I think the main advantage of extensive offshore experience is that it prepares one for the manic-depressive cycles almost everyone seems to go through on a long trip. Usually these cycles are synchronous, with all hands either full of beans or in the dumps at the same time, but it can happen that individual ups and downs occur out of phase. Either way it can be trying, less so when one expects it of oneself and of others.

What else of practical use is to be learned from long periods out of sight of land? Well, it turns out to be important to have chosen the right route and season and to have a sound vessel, worthy shipmates, plenty of tools and spares, good food, lots to read—an unremarkable list that can be formulated just as well in an armchair before the fire. So although all of us were glad Dixon was on board, in retrospect his chief contributions came from his competence rather than from his prior experience.

All watches were four hours long. The schedule was made out with two people per watch during the day and three at

229

To press a boat like Morgan-designed
60-foot Maredea *week after week*
in transatlantic race is experience
whose immediacy never fades.
Cruising passage across ocean is less
strenuous, permits shaping of
venture to suit abilities and
temperaments of crew.

night, the theory being that someone else would normally be up during the day to give a hand if needed. Everyone had eight consecutive hours off daily, and the composition of each watch changed constantly so that we were one crew and not two separate ones. Germaine and Ellen had only two watches per day to enable them to concentrate on the cuisine, which was kept to a high standard.

I stayed out of watch and was on call at all times, which was a good thing because nobody else was really familiar with all the details of running the ship. Even without this circumstance I think it is a good idea for the skipper to stay out of watch, since then he can view the proceedings with a certain amount of perspective and can serve as a fresh reserve without having to disturb the hands in the sack.

As it happened, the provision for three on the night watches was not necessary, since we did relatively little sail changing and never flew a spinnaker. Usually sail changes of any magnitude at night took place when the next watch came up. I am sure we could have made out very well with a total crew of five, or perhaps three couples if the ladies were as able and game as the two we had with us.

Quite apart from taking up less space and getting less in one another's way, a small crew has the advantage of enhancing the sense of accomplishment a long passage brings. "Less is more," said Mies van der Rohe in another connection, and provided there is a reserve against injury or illness, the same principle applies to the crew of an offshore cruiser.

We estimated that the passage would take about three weeks. The freezer and refrigerator on *Minots Light* are fortunately large enough to hold fresh food for seven people for three weeks, and we ate well. We also carried another three weeks' worth of canned and otherwise preserved food against the independent possibilities of catastrophe to the rig and catastrophe to the refrigeration system, plus still more in iron rations. I now believe we took too much. In fact, when we arrived in Scotland we still had on board more food and water than the race committee for the transatlantic race that took place later that summer would have required of us at the start.

We gave no special attention to the onions, potatoes, carrots, cabbages, green peppers, oranges, and apples we took, and they lasted the entire trip. Of course, we were careful to get good produce and it was fairly cold all the time, but fresh fruit and vegetables are so appreciated at sea that I would risk taking them in any circumstance. We brought twenty dozen eggs and, disregarding the advice of people who write books on cruising, we did not dip them in melted paraffin, pack them in salt, varnish them, or even turn them over, and when we ate the last ones four weeks later (with haggis, by the way, a delicious combination) they were perfectly good.

Water consumption averaged three quarts per person per day. Sea water was used for cooking vegetables and for washing dishes, and there was not a great deal of personal washing because of the persistent cold. Had the weather been warmer, more fresh water would have been used, but there was plenty to spare: 130 gallons when we arrived out of the 235 gallons we started with.

Everyone enjoyed sterilized whole milk, of which we took a hundred quart cans. It does not require refrigeration and has only a faint off-taste. For some reason this milk was extremely difficult to obtain. Until a week before we left the only firm that would sell me any was in California, and they supplied only gallon cans. Finally, by swearing a mighty oath of secrecy, I was able to get what I wanted from a dealer in New York. Another beverage much liked by all hands was apple juice, of which three cases— 27 gallons—vanished in two weeks despite the competition of the milk and of canned tomato, grapefruit, and orange juices.

While planning the passage I studied all the accounts of Atlantic crossings under sail I could find. When the average speeds of the various modern boats were expressed in terms of $\sqrt{\text{LWL}}$, the square roots of their waterline lengths expressed in feet, the results were surprisingly consistent. Transatlantic racers managed on the whole to make good a speed in knots of just about $\sqrt{\text{LWL}}$, whereas vessels cruising over made good a mean speed of about 75 percent of $\sqrt{\text{LWL}}$. On the average, then, an ocean cruiser of fairly recent vintage is only 25 percent slower than her racing cousin.

I say "only" because over a largely downwind course the ability to carry a spinnaker whenever possible is a big factor, as is the efficiency conferred by the large, expert crew of the racing boat. Lacking the spur of competition, with a crew probably half as large and twice as old, no doubt with last year's sails and winches and a hull older still, I think the performance of my list of cruisers was very good indeed.

The waterline length of *Minots Light* is a bit over 42 feet, so $\sqrt{\text{LWL}}$ equals 6.5 for her. Seventy-five percent of that is 4.9. Somewhere between 4.9 knots and 6.5 knots lay her probable average speed then, because we planned to use her diesel engine during calms to compensate for not pressing too hard during gales. In general we wanted to take it easy and to try to live well at sea, and we succeeded in both ambitions. In point of fact the engine was run for only thirty-six hours, about seven percent of the time, and nearly all of that was in short snatches to charge the batteries because of the demise of our generating set.

So, what with not much use of the engine and not working especially hard on deck, I was astonished to arrive at Oban, Scotland, barely twenty days out of Woods Hole. Our route covered 3,100 miles, and we averaged 154 miles per day for a mean speed of 6.4 knots, close to what we might have expected had we raced. The reason, of course, lay in the generally fair winds we had; even the gales cooperated.

We left Woods Hole late in May in a mild westerly and took our departure at 1630 from the whistler off No Mans Land south of Martha's Vineyard. During the night the wind backed to the southeast and headed us, and morning saw us close-hauled on the starboard tack. Long gray-green swells, some topped with white like Alpine peaks in summer, extended to the horizon in every direction. There was little conversation as the lassitude that marks incipient seasickness began to displace the euphoria of at last being clear of the shore after a winter of planning. The Atlantic was giving us an entrance exam, a trial by mild ordeal, to see if we and the ship were fit to continue across.

We must have passed the test, because the next day the wind veered to SSW

233

Opposite: Rod Stephens in Dorade *on way home across Atlantic after winning 1933* Fastnet Race. *Above: Long ocean races are planned so prevailing winds will be behind beam, and spinnakers are carried most of the time. Head winds may nevertheless be encountered.*

235

*On passage, a good meal and a snooze
are as important as a good day's run. Below:
Living well on* Minots Light *on calm
day. Center: Proper leeboards are essential
offshore. With large crews working hard,
eating is frequent during races. Bottom left:*
Men *of* Hother *take time for soup.
Right:* Barlovento II *during Bermuda Race.*

and the water temperature jumped from 49 degrees Fahrenheit to 68. We were in the Gulf Stream, and remained in it for three days with runs of over a hundred and eighty miles on all of them. I recall every detail of those days, the bright sun and blue sky, the steady swish of foam past the quarter, the occasional splash of warm water on a bare arm, the great joy of watching the Kenyon needle stay above eight for hours on end, the discovery of the competence of one's shipmates—altogether the one and only way for people to live.

Our strategy was to head southeast to latitude 40°N, keep along 40°N to 45°W or thereabouts, and then follow a great circle to Scotland. In this way we should stay clear of icebergs and the steamer lanes, yet still be able to expect westerly winds of some strength and consistency for much of the way. This was the course we actually followed, and indeed the winds were for the most part from the west.

Alas, they were from the northwest most of the time, not from the southwest as suggested by the pilot chart. So much the better, on the one hand, because this meant a reach instead of a dead run on the latter part of the passage. So much the worse, on the other hand, because northerly winds in early June are cold, cold, cold. Long woolen or quilted underwear was invariably worn at night and during most days as well, plus sweaters and jackets and hats and gloves. It was often difficult to squeeze through the main companionway.

Fortunately life in the cockpit was nearly always dry, partly because the ship is big and partly because of Dacron weather cloths laced to the after pulpit and to the lifelines on both sides of the cockpit. Occasionally, though, a special wave straight from Baffin Bay would sneak under the weather cloth and jump over the coaming to slither inside someone's oilies. The weather cloths also contributed to our morale in another way, quite unexpected. Every once in a while we became weary of the proximity of the sea; its frothy wet greenness just inches away got to be almost too much to bear. By sitting on the lee side of the cockpit only the weather cloth to windward could be seen, a pleasant change at times.

The first few days at sea are

crucial for the success of a voyage, I believe, since the attitudes of the crew toward one another and toward the voyage itself are set then. A happy ship can only develop when there is a general spirit of tolerance and goodwill despite the high population density, a common self-pruning of bulging egos to further the drive to get the best from the vessel. It is all too easy for a permanent feud to develop over a wet sock left on someone's pillow or for the helmsman on watch during dinner to acquire a permanent grouch when no hot biscuits are left for him. Good weather at the start of the voyage is a big help in this respect. We were fortunate to have three days of shirt-sleeve temperatures and fair winds in the Gulf Stream soon after we left Woods Hole. We settled down to our new way of life with little friction, and only to a minor extent did the discomfort brought by the northerly winds that came later upset the delicate equilibrium of personalities that was achieved at the beginning.

Early on the second week out of Woods Hole we were south of the Grand Banks. Monday, the third of June, was a windless day and the engine was run for ten hours in the afternoon and evening. It was pleasant to have nothing much to do for a change and to renew our acquaintanceships with one another. The log notes the sighting of two whales and a freighter, an involved dispute about exactly where the sun rises and why, and the baking of a splendid apple pie during which all hands tried a variety of sail combinations to hold the ship steady. A slight swell was beginning to appear and the sky was filling with light cloud—an ominous if muted sign of what was to come. About midnight a breeze came in from the northwest, and by noon Tuesday it had grown to a solid Force 6. We shortened down to genoa and mizzen staysail at 1540.

Genoa and mizzen staysail turned out to be a fine sail combination for broad reaching in a seaway. There is plenty of area, but being in light cloth it is easy to handle and there is no chafe nor any of the problems posed by main booms and spinnakers in such circumstances.

Early Tuesday evening the wind dropped somewhat, but we suspected a trick and, sure enough, by midnight its strength was up to Force 7 and at dawn it

Below: Francis Chichester at 69 leaves Plymouth, England, for single-handed Atlantic cruise in Robert Clark-designed staysail ketch Gipsy Moth V. *He averaged 155 miles per day. Bottom: Devon coast is welcome sight after Atlantic passage.*

was Force 8. As we roared along at over nine knots it began to rain and the barometer to drop, so when the mizzen staysail tack pennant let go we took in the staysail without argument. There was no detectable change in our speed. Soon the wind climbed still higher and we replaced the genoa with the storm jib and forestaysail. It was not a nice morning. At noon the wind veered to the northeast and moderated, and we set the mizzen to ease the steering. With storm jib, forestaysail, and mizzen we were as comfortable as possible, everything considered: that is, we were damned uncomfortable, but everything was under control and none of the sails was too large to cope with if the going happened to get worse.

For two more days the wind stayed at gale force, and we bashed along at an average of seven knots on a close reach, more or less on course. While all was well on deck, down below there was no relief from the motion and the constant racket did no good for the nerves. Moving from one place to another was an acrobatic feat. Still vivid in my memory is the sight of damp clothing hanging from the handrails in the deckhouse and main cabin, all of it swaying in counterpoint to the rolling of the ship. What with the Dacron leeboards also up in front of every berth, those below rarely saw one another, though every now and then an unexpected lurch would send a body crashing into one's lap as a reminder that one was not alone.

The incessant noise, in particular the vibration of the rigging, made conversation all but impossible. Not that any of us had anything to say apart from the few words needed now and then to keep the ship's routine going. We each knew what the others were thinking. Will it ever stop? How much more can the ship take before something lets go? How much more can I take before my will becomes too paralyzed for me to function?

I don't want to exaggerate our states of mind; neither panic nor catalepsy was at all imminent. Two things kept our morale at a reasonable level: *Minots Light* was standing up solidly to wind and sea, and we were going in the right direction. There was hope. Life went on.

Late Thursday the wind backed to the northwest and picked up still further. Enough was enough. Down came the forestaysail and mizzen with our unanimous approval, and down came our speed from eight knots to just half that under storm jib alone. The difference was amazing. We rode over the tumbling seas instead of crashing into them, no longer did green water cascade on deck, we could think without the violent motion dominating our consciousness. We emerged from our shells to become human beings again.

Dawn Friday saw winds that steadily diminished and we went more and more slowly, but nobody had the energy to put up more sail until the afternoon. It was a case of collective psychic exhaustion, not physical exhaustion, almost as if we were all in mild shock. The flame of adventure had flickered out in the storm and needed re-kindling. From noon Thursday to noon Friday we traveled only eighty-seven miles, the poorest run of the voyage by far.

This experience taught me that the emotional obstacles to getting sail back up at the right time after a prolonged storm are vastly more severe than the physical ones. In such a situation it is really worth making every effort to keep the community spirit high enough to get the ship sailing efficiently as soon as the weather permits.

Eventually the main, mizzen, and genoa were set and we changed course to 075°, the initial great circle course to Scotland, which cheered us up a little. Only a little, because the barometer was still falling, as it had been for five days, and we had no idea what to expect. We found out soon enough. Saturday night saw us down to jib topsail and mizzen, Force 7 from the northwest again, steep seas, and the further complication of shipping all around us as we crossed the steamer lanes. At 0200 Sunday two ships passed simultaneously almost within hailing distance, one to port and one to starboard, an unsettling experience. The term "steamer lane" is no figure of speech; ships seem to follow one another to and from Europe as if on the lanes of a highway.

The wind continued to blow strongly all day Sunday. Early Monday it fell to Force 6 and we put up the forestaysail and replaced the mizzen with the large mizzen staysail. That was the last we saw of truly nasty weather.

Actually, it was never really

With right shipmates and right ship, here 40-foot Concordia sloop Green Witch, *good days at sea are even better, bad days can be taken in stride. It is always sad when crew accustomed to working together must break up at end of voyage.*

unbearable at any time, and *Minots Light* behaved well, but the roar of wind and sea, the violent lurches, and the constant damp cold, day after day, were not much fun. Of these factors, the only one we might have controlled without sacrificing speed was the dampness and cold below deck. There are charcoal stoves in both main and after cabins that are quite adequate for this purpose, but we could not get them to draw during the storm. Trying to light them meant a cloud of smoke filling the interior. The secret seems to be to get the stoves going before the wind becomes too strong.

Nothing much happened from then on. To be more precise, many things happened, but it is not easy to capture in words just how vivid the banal events of life at sea seem at the time. To snatch a sun-sight in a cloudy sky after two days without one is high drama, and no denouement in the theater can match the figuring of the day's run. Coaxing half a knot more speed than the previous watch could is a feat to boast of loudly. To eat an honest-to-God steak with mashed potatoes (*real* mashed potatoes, not the plastic ones that come in envelopes) a thousand miles from land is a transcendent

experience, to be savored days in advance and days afterward.

One less pleasant event was the fracture of the tang that held the mizzen staysail halyard block. A gust hit us, and the whole works just fell down. Since this was our favorite sail, it was fortunate the incident occurred only the evening before we reached Scotland. I took the hint, and later that summer replaced the entire mizzen masthead assembly, originally of bronze, with a stronger one of stainless steel. The year before I had replaced the original main masthead assembly with a stainless one, but expert opinion had it that the mizzen was okay as it was. The incredible record of rigging failures at sea in recent years has done nothing to change my skepticism of expert opinion since then.

I had expected a lonely passage given our route, but it was not that way at all until the final week. For the first ten days we saw one or two ships daily, even though we were well south of the prescribed steamer lanes, and afterward, when we were north of them, only three or four more in all. The second day out a few U.S. Navy jets buzzed us at mast height, which was terrifying. I suppose they thought we might have been smuggling ICBM's to Cuba the hard way. We saw no other aircraft, but twice heard one pass overhead. It seems clear that if we had had to abandon ship without being able to make a radio distress call, we might have spent a long time in the life raft.

The spoor of civilization also pursued us, in the form of oil drums, mattresses, fish net floats, pieces of timber, and other debris. I am sorry to say we added to the permanent junk population of the sea to the extent of a dozen five-gallon polyethylene jugs which we started out with lashed on deck and filled with diesel oil. Despite all our efforts to keep them sealed they constantly leaked and, worse, managed to absorb sea water as well. A funnel with a very fine filter separated out most of the water when we refueled under way, but it was a terribly slow process and eventually we simply dumped the jugs overboard, oil and all.

If I ever take a deck load of fuel again I will do so in steel containers: better a little rust on deck than water in the fuel. Also, I will use a small electric pump to transfer the fuel to the tanks instead of trying to pour it directly. But I did something even more sens-

ible two years ago by installing an additional fuel tank to extend *Minots Light's* range under power to a thousand miles at her most economical speed.

On the other hand, plastic jugs are excellent for emergency water. They float when full of fresh water, which stays potable in them for long periods, and if they should strike someone when heaved over in abandoning ship they will do less harm than steel containers. We carried twenty gallons of water in four of these jugs stowed in the dinghy with a line tied to them ready to secure to the inflatable life raft in an emergency.

Our navigational routine was rather simple. We towed a log and kept track of our dead-reckoning position with reasonable care. Usually we were able to get both morning and noon sights, and if so we never bothered with anything else. The final two days were unfortunately overcast, just when we really wanted to know exactly where we were. I was able to get strong Consol signals from the stations at Bushmills in Northern Ireland and at Stavanger in Norway, but as Consol lines of position can be in error by as much as a dozen miles I was not too happy about relying upon them for a landfall.

At last the moment of truth came, 1500 on June 17, when my figures showed that Bloody Foreland, a high cliff at the northwest corner of Ireland, ought to be off the starboard beam. But nothing but low, gray clouds were in sight, matched by our low, gray spirits. Germaine claimed she detected the odor of land, but this was dismissed as wishful smelling. Obviously we were lost in the North Atlantic, and my feeble reassurance that we still had a month's supply of food and water comforted nobody.

Finally someone pointed to one of the clouds to starboard and said, "That cloud isn't moving."

He was right, and soon visibility improved enough for the whole coastline to be made out. Land! We were glad to see it, but our pleasure was subdued. Partly we felt the inevitable letdown at the end of any adventure, partly it was rather deflating to sail nearly three thousand miles to reach nothing more spectacular than a smudge on the horizon. No brass bands, no naked maidens swimming out to greet us, no nothing.

It began to rain as we changed course for Dubh Artach lighthouse off the entrance to the Firth of Lorne. After dark our return to civilization was confirmed by the appearance of a coaster from astern which tried its best to run us down. We bore off to starboard; he turned to starboard. We went hard over to port; he followed us to port. We turned on the spreader lights and shone a searchlight on his bridge, but all this seemed merely to encourage him. Finally, at the last minute, we jibed over and with the help of the engine got clear as he passed no more than a boat length (ours) away.

Our ruffled nerves were calmed at 0200 when the twin flashes of Dubh Artach appeared on schedule, and I experienced a marvelous feeling of contentment as we motored up the lovely Firth of Lorne in a flat calm soon afterward. To port was the green Isle of Mull, to starboard Colonsay, Jura, and then the mainland shore. A distant roar we later learned to have been the tide pouring violently through the fabled Gulf of Coirebhreacain (pronounced Corryvreckan), where it is said that once a destroyer unwisely passing through was turned bodily through 180 degrees by a whirlpool.

245

At 0800 we were in Oban, the destination chosen six months earlier. Almost at once we were presented with a matched pair of haggises, a copy of the Clyde Cruising Club's indispensable "Sailing Directions for the West Coast of Scotland," and an invitation to take hot baths. A customs officer came aboard, welcomed us to Scotland, and requested a document that, according to the British Consul in New York, had been abolished a year earlier. He said we would all have to return immediately to New York with the boat and get this document. We thought it the funniest joke imaginable, gave him a drink, and complimented him on his sense of humor—but to this day I am sure he was quite serious, and when he left he made straight for his office, no doubt to get reinforcements. We never saw him again.

A fine town, Oban, with cheerful people who live in a pleasant setting—but it was all anticlimax there after three weeks at sea.

In comparing notes with several of my erstwhile shipmates years afterward, I found quite different recollections of the voyage. To some the dominant memory was of the periods of splendid sailing when we and the ship were as one, to others it was of cold and general discomfort. On a personal level, nobody had been entirely happy with the personalities of all of his comrades, perhaps least of all with mine. But everybody was without question glad to have come, and felt a different person in some way for having done so.

My perspective was different, partly because I had been the skipper and partly because I had had more experience of expedition living than the others. I had been unnecessarily anxious for much of the trip, which had taken the edge off my enjoyment of the better moments and did nothing to make me good company. My real satisfaction came at the end. To me it was significant that we had done exactly what we had set out to do, and had arrived in Oban with the ship and our amity still intact. I had survived far rougher passages and been a member of far less harmonious crews to complain on either score. What stood out most of all—and still does—is that I had sailed across the Atlantic, a long-held dream that lost nothing in the process of becoming reality.

Bibliography

Bavier, Robert N., Jr., *A View from the Cockpit,* New York, Dodd, Mead & Company, 1966. *Constellation's* defense of the America's Cup in 1965 from the perspective of her helmsman.

Bradford, Ernle, *The Wind off the Island,* New York, Harcourt, Brace, and World, 1960. A year on the Sicilian coast in the 30-foot leeboard sloop *Mother Goose.*

Chichester, Francis, *Gipsy Moth Circles the World,* London, Hodder and Stoughton, 1967. Chichester was sixty-five when he made this single-handed voyage in a 53-foot ketch.

Ellam, Patrick, and Mudie, Colin, *Sopranino,* London, Rupert Hart-Davis, 1958. A 10,000-mile cruise in a 20-foot cutter.

Elvström, Paul, *Elvström Speaks,* Lymington, Nautical Publishing Company, 1969. Lively recollections of the Danish master small-boat sailor and four-time Olympic champion.

Fox, Uffa, *Sailing, Seamanship, and Yacht Construction,* London, Peter Davies, 1934. Not really a textbook despite its title, this exuberant survey of every aspect of the sailor's world will never lose its freshness.

Gann, Ernest K., *Song of the Sirens,* New York, Simon and Schuster, 1968. Mainly about the author's love affair with the schooner *Albatros.*

Hiscock, Eric C., *Beyond the West Horizon,* New York, Oxford University Press, 1963. The second circumnavigation by the extremely competent author and his wife in the 30-foot sloop *Wanderer III.*

Johnson, Irving and Electa, *Yankee Sails Across Europe,* New York, W. W. Norton & Company, 1962. Sailing and canalling in the 51-foot centerboard ketch *Yankee.*

Lewis, David, *Daughters of the Wind,* London, Victor Gollancz, 1967. A passage from England to New Zealand in the 40-foot catamaran *Rehu Moana* via the Straits of Magellan.

MacCullagh, Richard, *Vikings' Wake,* Princeton, D. Van Nostrand Company. Successful attempt to capture "the spirit of a joyous voyage in sail amidst the friendly people of the Danish isles."

Millar, George, *A White Boat from England,* New York, Alfred A. Knopf, 1952. Beautifully-written account of a passage from England to the Mediterranean by the author and his wife in the 45-foot sloop *Serica;* a classic.

Mitchell, Carleton, *Passage East,* London, John Murray, 1954. The 1952 Transatlantic Race as experienced in the 57-foot yawl *Caribee.*

Pye, Peter, *A Sail in a Forest,* London, Rupert Hart-Davis, 1961. Pleasant tale of a cruise to Finland in the 29-foot gaff cutter *Moonraker.*

Robinson, Bill, *Over the Horizon,* Princeton, D. Van Nostrand Company, 1966. Fourteen cruises in waters ranging from Long Island Sound to the Fijis.

Robinson, William Albert, *To the Great Southern Sea,* New York, Harcourt, Brace & Company, 1956. South Pacific cruise in the magnificent 70-foot brigantine *Varua.*

Slocum, Joshua, *The Voyages of Joshua Slocum,* New Brunswick, Rutgers University Press, 1958. All of Slocum's writings, including his masterpiece, *Sailing Alone Around the World,* with notes by Walter Magnes Teller.

Smeeton, Miles, *Once Is Enough,* New York, W. W. Norton & Company, 1959. From Australia to Chile in the 46-foot ketch *Tzu Hang,* which was overturned twice in great storms.

Snaith, William, *Across the Western Ocean,* London, Macmillan, 1966. Racing and cruising across the Atlantic in the 47-foot yawl *Figaro;* Snaith tells it like it is, and then some.

Tabarly, Eric, *Lonely Victory,* London, Souvenir Press, 1965. The single-handed Transatlantic Race of 1964 aboard the 44-foot ketch *Pen Duick II.*

Tangvald, Peter, *Sea Gypsy,* London, William Kimber, 1966. Around the world in the 32-foot cutter *Dorothea* with a man not barnacled by inhibition or modesty.

Tilman, H. W., *Mischief in Patagonia,* New York, Cambridge University Press, 1957. The first of Tilman's remarkable voyages in the 45-foot gaff cutter *Mischief.*

Index

Picture references in italics